THE DESECULARIZATION OF THE WORLD

PETER L. BERGER is University Professor and director of the Institute for the Study of Economic Culture at Boston University. Among the books he has written are *A Far Glory: The Quest
for Faith in an Age of Credulity*, *Redeeming Laughter*, and *A Rumor of
Angels: Modern Society and the Rediscovery of the Supernatural*.

THE DESECULARIZATION OF THE WORLD

Resurgent Religion and World Politics

Edited by Peter L. Berger

Peter L. Berger   Tu Weiming

Jonathan Sacks   George Weigel

David Martin   Grace Davie

Abdullahi A. An-Na'im

Ethics and Public Policy Center
Washington, D.C.

William B. Eerdmans Publishing Company
Grand Rapids, Michigan

Copyright © 1999 by the Ethics and Public Policy Center
1015 Fifteenth St. N.W., Washington, D.C. 20005

Published jointly 1999 by the Ethics and Public Policy Center and
Wm. B. Eerdmans Publishing Co.
255 Jefferson Ave. S.E., Grand Rapids, Mich. 49503

Printed in the United States of America

04 03   7 6 5 4

Library of Congress Cataloging-in-Publication Data

The desecularization of the world: resurgent religion and world politics /
edited by Peter L. Berger.
p.   cm.
Includes bibliographical references.
ISBN 0-8028-4691-2 (pbk.: alk. paper)
1. Religion and politics Congresses. 2. Secularism Congresses.
I. Berger, Peter L.
BL65.P7D47   1999
291.1'77'09 — dc21   99-32103
CIP

Contents

Preface

In 1996 John Kizer, president of the Greve Foundation, approached Andrew Bacevich with an idea. Bacevich was then executive director of the Foreign Policy Institute at the Nitze School of Advanced International Studies at Johns Hopkins University. The news, Kizer said, was filled with reports of the impact of religion on politics: the evangelical upsurge in Latin America, Muslim-Christian rivalries in Africa, disputes between Arabs and Israelis, secularist-religious struggles in Turkey, Muslim fundamentalists fighting a secularizing military in Algeria, Hindu fundamentalists beating the Congress Party in India. How about taking a longer look at these phenomena to see how religion is likely to influence politics in the coming century?

Accepting the challenge, Professor Bacevich consulted us at the Ethics and Public Policy Center, where the impact of religion on public life is a central concern. Could the Nitze School and the Center together launch a lecture series on this subject, attempting to cover the main religions and regions of the world? We quickly roped in Professor Peter Berger of Boston University, perhaps the world's leading sociologist of religion: would he help us think through the project and choose the speakers, and would he deliver the first lecture himself? He agreed to do so, and we began our work.

The product of that joint effort is presented in this volume, whose title is taken from Professor Berger's powerful keynote lecture. We were fortunate to be able to recruit as lecturers some of the leading students of religion and politics in the world: Tu Weiming, the director of the Harvard-Yenching Institute; Jonathan Sacks, the chief rabbi of Britain and the Commonwealth; George Weigel, my predecessor at the Center and the author of a forthcoming biography of Pope John Paul II; David Martin, the leading student of the evangelical upsurge in the Third World; Grace Davie, a British sociologist who is an expert on religion in Europe; and Abdullahi An-Na'im, an internationally recognized scholar of Islam and human rights. We owe a debt of gratitude to our seven authors, for traveling to Washington to speak and for the additional work they did to prepare their papers for publication.

I would like as well to thank Professor Bacevich for asking us to collaborate with him, always a task both intellectually stimulating and personally rewarding. On his behalf and my own, I wish to thank John Kizer and the Greve Foundation for his initiative, his counsel throughout, and the foundation's financial support. Finally, these essays were edited for publication by Carol Griffith, editor at the Ethics and Public Policy Center, to whom we at the Center and all who read this book are in debt.

Elliott Abrams, *President*
Ethics and Public Policy Center

The Desecularization of the World: A Global Overview

Peter L. Berger

A few years ago the first volume coming out of the so-called Fundamentalism Project landed on my desk. The Fundamentalism Project was very generously funded by the MacArthur Foundation and chaired by Martin Marty, the distinguished church historian at the University of Chicago. A number of very reputable scholars took part in it, and the published results are of generally excellent quality. But my contemplation of this first volume gave me what has been called an "*aha!* experience." The book was very big, sitting there on my desk—a "book-weapon," the kind that could do serious injury. So I asked myself, why would the MacArthur Foundation shell out several million dollars to support an international study of religious fundamentalists?

Two answers came to mind. The first was obvious and not very interesting. The MacArthur Foundation is a very progressive outfit; it

---

Peter L. Berger is University Professor and director of the Institute for the Study of Economic Culture at Boston University. Among the books he has written are *A Far Glory: The Quest for Faith in an Age of Credulity* (1992) and *Redeeming Laughter* (1997). This essay is adapted with permission from the original article, which appeared in *The National Interest* (no. 46, Winter 1996/ 97; Washington, D.C.).

understands fundamentalists to be anti-progressive; the Project, then, was a matter of knowing one's enemies. But there was also a more interesting answer. "Fundamentalism" is considered a strange, hard-to-understand phenomenon; the purpose of the Project was to delve into this alien world and make it more understandable. But to whom? *Who* finds this world strange? Well, the answer to *that* question was easy: people to whom the officials of the MacArthur Foundation normally talk, such as professors at elite American universities. And with this came the aha! experience. The concern that must have led to this Project was based on an upside-down perception of the world, according to which "fundamentalism" (which, when all is said and done, usually refers to any sort of passionate religious movement) is a rare, hard-to-explain thing. But a look either at history or at the contemporary world reveals that what is rare is not the phenomenon itself but knowledge of it. The difficult-to-understand phenomenon is not Iranian mullahs but American university professors—it might be worth a multi-million-dollar project to try to explain that!

Mistakes of Secularization Theory

My point is that the assumption that we live in a secularized world is false. The world today, with some exceptions to which I will come presently, is as furiously religious as it ever was, and in some places more so than ever. This means that a whole body of literature by historians and social scientists loosely labeled "secularization theory" is essentially mistaken. In my early work I contributed to this literature. I was in good company—most sociologists of religion had similar views, and we had good reasons for holding them. Some of the writings we produced still stand up. (As I like to tell my students, one advantage of being a social scientist, as against being, say, a philosopher or a theologian, is that you can have as much fun when your theories are falsified as when they are verified!)

Although the term "secularization theory" refers to works from the 1950s and 1960s, the key idea of the theory can indeed be traced to the Enlightenment. That idea is simple: Modernization necessarily leads to a decline of religion, both in society and in the minds of individuals. And it is precisely this key idea that has turned out to be wrong. To be sure, modernization has had some secularizing effects, more in some places than in others. But it has also provoked powerful movements of counter-secularization. Also, secularization on the societal level is not necessarily linked to secularization on the level of individual consciousness. Certain religious institutions have lost power and influence in many societies, but both old and new religious beliefs and practices have nevertheless continued in the lives of individuals, sometimes taking new institutional forms and sometimes leading to great explosions of religious fervor. Conversely, religiously identified institutions can play social or political roles even when very few people believe or practice the religion that the institutions represent. To say the least, the relation between religion and modernity is rather complicated.

The proposition that modernity necessarily leads to a decline of religion is, in principle, "value free." That is, it can be affirmed both by people who think it is good news and by people who think it is very bad news. Most Enlightenment thinkers and most progressive-minded people ever since have tended toward the idea that secularization is a good thing, at least insofar as it does away with religious phenomena that are "backward," "superstitious," or "reactionary" (a religious residue purged of these negative characteristics may still be deemed acceptable). But religious people, including those with very traditional or orthodox beliefs, have also affirmed the modernity/secularity linkage, and have greatly bemoaned it. Some have then defined modernity as the enemy, to be fought whenever possible. Others have, on the contrary, seen modernity as some kind of invincible world-view to which religious beliefs and practices should adapt themselves. In other words, *rejection* and *adaptation* are two strategies open to religious communities in a world understood to be secularized. As is always the case when strategies are based on mistaken perceptions of the terrain, both strategies have had very doubtful results.

It is possible, of course, to reject any number of modern ideas and values theoretically, but making this rejection stick in the lives of people is much harder. To do that requires one of two strategies. The first is *religious revolution:* one tries to take over society as a whole and make one's counter-modern religion obligatory for everyone—a difficult enterprise in most countries in the contemporary world.

(Franco tried in Spain and failed; the mullahs are still at it in Iran and a couple of other places.) And this *does* have to do with modernization, which brings about very heterogeneous societies and a quantum leap in intercultural communication, two factors favoring pluralism and *not* favoring the establishment (or reestablishment) of religious monopolies. The other possible way of getting people to reject modern ideas and values in their lives is to create *religious subcultures* designed to keep out the influences of the outside society. That is a somewhat more promising exercise than religious revolution, but it too is fraught with difficulty. Modern culture is a very powerful force, and an immense effort is required to maintain enclaves with an airtight defense system. Ask the Amish in eastern Pennsylvania. Or ask a Hasidic rabbi in the Williamsburg section of Brooklyn.

Interestingly, secularization theory has also been falsified by the results of adaptation strategies by religious institutions. If we really lived in a highly secularized world, then religious institutions could be expected to survive to the degree that they manage to adapt to secularity. That has been the empirical assumption of adaptation strategies. What has in fact occurred is that, by and large, religious communities have survived and even flourished to the degree that they have *not* tried to adapt themselves to the alleged requirements of a secularized world. To put it simply, experiments with secularized religion have generally failed; religious movements with beliefs and practices dripping with reactionary supernaturalism (the kind utterly beyond the pale at self-respecting faculty parties) have widely succeeded.

The Catholic Church vs. Modernity

The struggle with modernity in the Roman Catholic Church nicely illustrates the difficulties of various strategies. In the wake of the Enlightenment and its multiple revolutions, the initial response by the Church was militant and then defiant rejection. Perhaps the most magnificent moment of that defiance came in 1870, when the First Vatican Council solemnly proclaimed the infallibility of the Pope and the immaculate conception of Mary, literally in the face of the Enlightenment about to occupy Rome in the shape of the army of Victor Emmanuel I. (The disdain was mutual. If you have ever visited the Roman monument to the Bersaglieri, the elite army units that occupied the Eternal City in the name of the Italian *Risorgimento,* you may have noticed the placement of the heroic figure in his Bersaglieri uniform—he is positioned so that his behind points exactly toward the Vatican.)

The Second Vatican Council, almost a hundred years later, considerably modified this rejectionist stance, guided as it was by the notion of *aggiornamento,* bringing the Church up to date—that is, up to date with the modern world. (I remember asking a Protestant theologian what he thought would happen at the Council—this was before it had convened; he replied that he didn't know but he was sure they would not read the minutes of the last meeting!) The Second Vatican Council was supposed to open windows, specifically the windows of the Catholic subculture that had been constructed when it became clear that the overall society could not be reconquered. In the United States, this Catholic subculture has been quite impressive right up to the very recent past. The trouble with opening windows is that you can't control what comes in, and a lot has come in—indeed, the whole turbulent world of modern culture—that has been very troubling to the Church. Under the current pontificate the Church has been steering a nuanced course between rejection and adaptation, with mixed results in different countries.

This is as good a point as any to mention that all my observations here are intended to be "value free"; that is, I am trying to look at the current religious scene objectively. For the duration of this exercise I have put aside my own religious beliefs. As a sociologist of religion, I find it probable that Rome had to do some reining in on the level of both doctrine and practice, in the wake of the institutional disturbances that followed Vatican II. To say this, however, in no way implies my theological agreement with what has been happening in the Roman Catholic Church under the present pontificate. Indeed, if I were Roman Catholic, I would have considerable misgivings about these developments. But I am a liberal Protestant (the adjective refers to my religious position and not to my politics), and I have no immediate existential stake in what is happening within the Roman community. I am speaking here as a sociologist, in which capacity I can claim a certain competence; I have no theological credentials.

THE GLOBAL RELIGIOUS SCENE

On the international religious scene, it is conservative or orthodox or traditionalist movements that are on the rise almost everywhere. These movements are precisely the ones that rejected an *aggiornamento* with modernity as defined by progressive intellectuals. Conversely, religious movements and institutions that have made great efforts to conform to a perceived modernity are almost everywhere on the decline. In the United States this has been a much commented upon fact, exemplified by the decline of so-called mainline Protestantism and the concomitant rise of Evangelicalism; but the United States is by no means unusual in this.

Nor is Protestantism. The conservative thrust in the Roman Catholic Church under John Paul II has borne fruit in both number of converts and renewed enthusiasm among native Catholics, especially in non-Western countries. Following the collapse of the Soviet Union there occurred a remarkable revival of the Orthodox Church in Russia. The most rapidly growing Jewish groups, both in Israel and in the Diaspora, are Orthodox. There have been similarly vigorous upsurges of conservative religion in all the other major religious communities—Islam, Hinduism, Buddhism—as well as revival movements in smaller communities (such as Shinto in Japan and Sikhism in India). These developments differ greatly in their social and political implications. What they have in common is their unambiguously *religious* inspiration. Consequently, taken together they provide a massive falsification of the idea that modernization and secularization are cognate phenomena. At the very least they show that *counter*-secularization is at least as important a phenomenon in the contemporary world as secularization.

Both in the media and in scholarly publications, these movements are often subsumed under the category of "fundamentalism." This is not a felicitous term, not only because it carries a pejorative undertone but also because it derives from the history of American Protestantism, where it has a specific reference that is distortive if extended to other religious traditions. All the same, the term has some suggestive use if one wishes to explain the aforementioned developments. It suggests a combination of several features—great religious passion, a defiance of what others have defined as the *Zeitgeist,* and a return to traditional sources of religious authority. These are indeed common features across cultural boundaries. And they do reflect the presence of secularizing forces, since they must be understood as a reaction *against* those forces. (In that sense, at least, something of the old secularization theory may be said to hold up, in a rather back-handed way.) This interplay of secularizing and counter-secularizing forces is, I would contend, one of the most important topics for a sociology of contemporary religion, but far too large to consider here. I can only drop a hint: Modernity, for fully understandable reasons, undermines all the old certainties; uncertainty is a condition that many people find very hard to bear; therefore, any movement (not only a religious one) that promises to provide or to renew certainty has a ready market.

Differences Among Thriving Movements

While the aforementioned common features are important, an analysis of the social and political impact of the various religious upsurges must also take full account of their differences. This becomes clear when one looks at what are arguably the two most dynamic religious upsurges in the world today, the Islamic and the Evangelical; the comparison also underlines the weakness of the category of "fundamentalism" as applied to both.

The Islamic upsurge, because of its more immediately obvious political ramifications, is better known. Yet it would be a serious error to see it only through a political lens. It is an impressive revival of emphatically *religious* commitments. And it is of vast geographical scope, affecting every single Muslim country from North Africa to Southeast Asia. It continues to gain converts, especially in sub-Saharan Africa (where it is often in head-on competition with Christianity). It is becoming very visible in the burgeoning Muslim communities in Europe and, to a much lesser extent, in North America. Everywhere it is bringing about a restoration, not only of Islamic beliefs but of distinctively Islamic life-styles, which in many ways directly contradict modern ideas—such as ideas about the relation of religion and the state, the role of women, moral codes of everyday behavior, and the boundaries of religious and moral tolerance. The Islamic revival is by no means restricted to the less modernized or "backward" sectors of society, as progressive intellectuals still like to think. On the contrary, it is very strong in cities with a high degree of modernization, and in a number of countries it is particularly visible among people with Western-style higher education—in Egypt and Turkey, for example, many daughters of secularized professionals are putting on the veil and other accoutrements of Islamic modesty.

Yet there are also great differences within the movement. Even within the Middle East, the Islamic heartland, there are both religiously and politically important differences between Sunni and Shiite revivals—Islamic conservatism means very different things in, say, Saudi Arabia and Iran. Away from the Middle East, the differences become even greater. Thus in Indonesia, the most populous Muslim country in the world, a very powerful revival movement, the Nudhat'ul-Ulama, is avowedly pro-democracy and pro-pluralism, the very opposite of what is commonly viewed as Muslim "fundamentalism." Where the political circumstances allow this, there is in many places a lively discussion about the relation of Islam to various modern realities, and there are sharp disagreements among individuals who are equally committed to a revitalized Islam. Still, for reasons deeply grounded in the core of the tradition, it is probably fair to say that, on the whole, Islam has had a difficult time coming to terms with key modern institutions, such as pluralism, democracy, and the market economy.

The Evangelical upsurge is just as breathtaking in scope. Geographically that scope is even wider. It has gained huge numbers of converts in East Asia—in all the Chinese communities (including, despite severe persecution, mainland China) and in South Korea, the Philippines, across the South Pacific, throughout sub-Saharan Africa (where it is often synthetized with elements of traditional African religion), apparently in parts of ex-Communist Europe. But the most remarkable success has occurred in Latin America; there are now thought to be between forty and fifty million Evangelical Protestants south of the U.S. border, the great majority of them first-generation Protestants. The most numerous component within the Evangelical upsurge is Pentecostalism, which combines biblical orthodoxy and a rigorous morality with an ecstatic form of worship and an emphasis on spiritual healing. Especially in Latin America, conversion to Protestantism brings about a cultural transformation—new attitudes toward work and consumption, a new educational ethos, and a violent rejection of traditional *machismo* (women play a key role in the Evangelical churches).

The origins of this worldwide Evangelical upsurge are in the United States, from which the missionaries first went out. But it is very important to understand that, virtually everywhere and emphatically in Latin America, this new Evangelicalism is thoroughly indigenous and no longer dependent on support from U.S. fellow believers—indeed, Latin American Evangelicals have been sending missionaries to the Hispanic community in this country, where there has been a comparable flurry of conversions.

Needless to say, the religious contents of the Islamic and Evangelical revivals are totally different. So are the social and political consequences (of which I will say more later). But the two developments also differ in another very important respect: The Islamic movement is occurring primarily in countries that are already Muslim or among Muslim emigrants (as in Europe), while the Evangelical movement is growing dramatically throughout the world in countries where this type of religion was previously unknown or very marginal.

Exceptions to the Desecularization Thesis

Let me, then, repeat what I said a while back: The world today is massively religious, is *anything but* the secularized world that had been predicted (whether joyfully or despondently) by so many analysts of modernity. There are, however, two exceptions to this proposition, one somewhat unclear, the other very clear.

The first apparent exception is Europe—more specifically, Europe west of what used to be called the Iron Curtain (the developments in the formerly Communist countries are as yet very under-researched and unclear). In Western Europe, if nowhere else, the old secularization theory would seem to hold. With increasing modernization there has been an increase in key indicators of secularization, both on the level of expressed beliefs (especially those that could be called orthodox in Protestant or Catholic terms) and, dramatically, on the level of church-related behavior—attendance at services of worship, adherence to church-dictated codes of personal behavior (especially with regard to sexuality, reproduction, and marriage), recruitment to the clergy. These phenomena, long observed in the northern countries of the continent, have since World War II rapidly engulfed the south. Thus Italy and Spain have experienced a rapid decline in church-related religion. So has Greece, thereby undercutting the claim of Catholic conservatives that Vatican II is to be blamed for the decline. There is now a massively secular Euro-culture, and what has happened in the south can be simply described (though not thereby explained) by that culture's invasion of these countries. It is not fanciful to predict that there will be similar developments in Eastern Europe, precisely to the degree that these countries too will be integrated into the new Europe.

While these facts are not in dispute, a number of recent works in the sociology of religion, notably in France, Britain, and Scandinavia, have questioned the term "secularization" as applied to these developments. A body of data indicates strong survivals of religion, most of it generally Christian in nature, despite the widespread alienation from the organized churches. A shift in the institutional location of religion, then, rather than secularization, would be a more accurate description of the European situation. All the same, Europe stands out as quite different from other parts of the world, and certainly from the United States. One of the most interesting puzzles in the sociology of religion is why Americans are so much more religious *as well as* more churchly than Europeans.

The other exception to the desecularization thesis is less ambiguous. There exists an international subculture composed of people with Western-type higher education, especially in the humanities and social sciences, that is indeed secularized. This subculture is the principal "carrier" of progressive, Enlightened beliefs and values. While its members are relatively thin on the ground, they are very influential, as they control the institutions that provide the "official" definitions of reality, notably the educational system, the media of mass communication, and the higher reaches of the legal system. They are remarkably similar all over the world today, as they have been for a long time (though, as we have seen, there are also defectors from this subculture, especially in the Muslim countries). Again, regrettably, I cannot speculate here as to why people with this type of education should be so prone to secularization. I can only point out that what we have here is a globalized *elite* culture.

In country after country, then, religious upsurges have a strongly populist character. Over and beyond the purely religious motives, these are movements of protest and resistance *against* a secular elite. The so-called culture war in the United States emphatically shares this feature. I may observe in passing that the plausibility of secularization theory owes much to this international subculture. When intellectuals travel, they usually touch down in intellectual circles—that is, among people much like themselves. They can easily fall into the misconception that these people reflect the overall visited society, which, of course, is a big mistake. Picture a secular intellectual from Western Europe socializing with colleagues at the faculty club of the University of Texas. He may think he is back home. But then picture him trying to drive through the traffic jam on Sunday morning in downtown Austin—or, heaven help him, turning on his car radio! What happens then is a severe jolt of what anthropologists call culture shock.

RESURGENT RELIGION: ORIGINS AND PROSPECTS

After this somewhat breathless *tour d'horizon* of the global religious scene, let me turn to some the questions posed for discussion in this set of essays. *First, what are the origins of the worldwide resurgence of religion?* Two possible answers have already been mentioned. One: Modernity tends to undermine the taken-for-granted certainties by which people lived through most of history. This is an uncomfortable state of affairs, for many an intolerable one, and religious movements that claim to give certainty have great appeal. Two: A purely secular view of reality has its principal social location in an elite culture that, not surprisingly, is resented by large numbers of people who are not part of it but who feel its influence (most troublingly, as their children are subjected to an education that ignores or even directly attacks their own beliefs and values). Religious movements with a strongly anti-secular bent can therefore appeal to people with resentments that sometimes have quite non-religious sources.

But I would refer once more to the little story with which I began, about American foundation officials worried about "fundamentalism." In one sense, there is nothing to explain here. Strongly felt religion has always been around; what needs explanation is its absence rather than its presence. Modern secularity is a much more puzzling phenomenon than all these religious explosions—if you will, the University of Chicago is a more interesting topic for the sociology of religion than the Islamic schools of Qom. In other words, the phenomena under consideration here on one level simply serve to demonstrate continuity in the place of religion in human experience.

Second, what is the likely future course of this religious resurgence? Given the considerable variety of important religious movements in the contemporary world, it would make little sense to venture a global prognosis. Predictions, if one dares to make them at all, will be more useful if applied to much narrower situations. One prediction, though, can be made with some assurance: There is no reason to think the world of the twenty-first century will be any less religious than the world is today. A minority of sociologists of religion have been trying to salvage the old secularization theory by what I would call the last-ditch thesis: Modernization *does* secularize, and movements like the Islamic and the Evangelical ones represent last-ditch defenses by religion that cannot last; eventually, secularity will triumph—or, to put it less respectfully, eventually Iranian mullahs, Pentecostal preachers, and Tibetan lamas will all think and act like professors of literature at American universities. I find this thesis singularly unpersuasive.

Having made this general prediction—that the world of the next century will not be less religious than the world of today—I will have to speculate very differently regarding different sectors of the religious scene. For example, I think that the most militant Islamic movements will find it hard to maintain their present stance *vis-à-vis* modernity once they succeed in taking over the governments of their countries (this, it seems, is already happening in Iran). I also think that Pentecostalism, as it exists today among mostly poor and uneducated people, is unlikely to retain its present religious and moral characteristics unchanged, as many of these people experience upward social mobility (this has already been observed extensively in the United States). Generally, many of these religious movements are linked to non-religious forces of one sort or another, and the future course of the former will be at least partially determined by the course of the latter. In the United States, for instance, militant Evangelicalism will have a different future course if some of its causes succeed in the political and legal arenas than if it continues to be frustrated in these arenas. Also, in religion as in every other area of human endeavor, individual personalities play a much larger role than most social scientists and historians are willing to concede. There might have been an Islamic revolution in Iran without the Ayatollah Khomeini, but it would probably have looked quite different. No one can predict the appearance of charismatic figures who will launch powerful religious movements in unexpected places. Who knows—perhaps the next religious upsurge in America will occur among disenchanted post-modernist academics!

Third, do the resurgent religions differ in their critique of the secular order? Yes, of course they do, depending on their particular belief systems. Cardinal Ratzinger and the Dalai Lama will be troubled by different aspects of contemporary secular culture. What both will agree upon, however, is the shallowness of a culture that tries to get along without any transcendent points of reference. And they will have good reasons to support this view. The religious impulse, the quest for meaning that transcends the restricted space of empirical existence in this world, has been a perennial feature of humanity. (This is not a theological statement but an anthropological one—an agnostic or even an atheist philosopher may well agree with it.) It would require something close to a mutation of the species to extinguish this impulse for good. The more radical thinkers of the Enlightenment and their more recent intellectual descendants hoped for something like this, of course. So far it has not happened, and as I have argued, it is unlikely to happen in the foreseeable future. The critique of secularity common to all the resurgent movements is that human existence bereft of transcendence is an impoverished and finally untenable condition.

To the extent that secularity today has a specifically modern form (there were earlier forms in, for example, versions of Confucianism and Hellenistic culture), the critique of secularity also entails a critique of at least these aspects of modernity. Beyond that, however, different religious movements differ in their relation to modernity. As I have said, an argument can be made that the Islamic resurgence strongly tends toward a negative view of modernity; in places it is downright anti-modern or counter-modernizing, as in its view of the role of women. By contrast, I think it can be shown that the Evangelical resurgence is positively modernizing in most places where it occurs, clearly so in Latin America. The new Evangelicals throw aside many of the traditions that have been obstacles to modernization—*machismo,* for one, and also the subservience to hierarchy that has been endemic to Iberian Catholicism. Their churches encourage values and behavior patterns that contribute to modernization. To take just one important case in point: In order to participate fully in the life of their congregations, Evangelicals will want to read the Bible; this desire to read the Bible encourages literacy and, beyond this, a positive attitude toward education and self-improvement. They also will want to be able to join in the discussion of congregational affairs, since those matters are largely in the hands of laypersons (indeed, largely in the hands of women); this lay operation of churches necessitates training in administrative skills, including the conduct of public meetings and the keeping of financial accounts. It is not fanciful to suggest that in this way Evangelical congregations serve—inadvertently, to be sure—as schools for democracy and for social mobility.

RELIGIOUS RESURGENCE AND WORLD AFFAIRS

Other questions posed for discussion in this volume concern the relation of the religious resurgence to a number of issues not linked to religion.

▪ First, *international politics.* Here one comes up head-on against the thesis, eloquently proposed not long ago by Samuel Huntington, that, with the end of the Cold War, international affairs will be affected by a "clash of civilizations" rather than by ideological conflicts. There is something to be said for this thesis. The great ideological conflict that animated the Cold War is certainly dormant for the moment, but I, for one, would not bet on its final demise. Nor can we be sure that new ideological conflicts may not arise in the future. To the extent that nationalism is an ideology (more accurately, each nationalism has its *own* ideology), ideology is alive and well in a long list of countries.

It is also plausible that, in the absence of the overarching confrontation between Soviet Communism and the American-led West, cultural animosities suppressed during the Cold War period are surfacing. Some of these animosities have themselves taken on an ideological form, as in the assertion of a distinctive Asian identity by a number of governments and intellectual groups in East and Southeast Asia. This ideology has become especially visible in debates over the allegedly ethnocentric/Eurocentric character of human rights as propagated by the United States and other Western governments and governmental organizations. But it would probably be an exaggeration to see these debates as signaling a clash of civilizations. The situation closest to a religiously defined clash of civilizations would come about if the world-view of the most radical branches of the Islamic resurgence came to be established within a wider spectrum of countries and became the basis of the foreign policies of these countries. As yet this has not happened.

To assess the role of religion in international politics, it would be useful to distinguish between political movements that are genuinely inspired by religion and those that use religion as a convenient legitimation for political agendas based on quite non-religious interests. Such a distinction is difficult but not impossible. Thus there is no reason to doubt that the suicide bombers of the Islamic Haws movement truly believe in the religious motives they avow. By contrast, there is good reason to doubt that the three parties involved in the Bosnian conflict, commonly represented as a clash between religions, are really inspired by religious ideas. I think it was P. J. O'Rourke who observed that these three parties are of the same race, speak the same language, and are distinguished only by their religion, which none of them believe. The same skepticism about the religious nature of an allegedly religious conflict is expressed in the following joke from Northern Ireland: As a man walks down a dark street in Belfast, a gunman jumps out of a doorway, holds a gun to his head, and asks, "Are you Protestant or Catholic?" The man stutters, "Well, actually, I'm an atheist." "Ah yes," says the gunman, "but are you a Protestant or a Catholic atheist?"

■ Second, *war and peace*. It would be nice to be able to say that religion is everywhere a force for peace. Unfortunately, it is not. Very probably religion in the modern world more often fosters war, both between and within nations. Religious institutions and movements are fanning wars and civil wars on the Indian subcontinent, in the Balkans, in the Middle East, and in Africa, to mention only the most obvious cases. Occasionally, indeed, religious institutions try to resist warlike policies or to mediate between conflicting parties. The Vatican mediated successfully in some international disputes in Latin America. There have been religiously inspired peace movements in several countries (including the United States, during the Vietnam War). Both Protestant and Catholic clergy have tried to mediate the conflict in Northern Ireland, though with notable lack of success.

But it is probably a mistake to look here simply at the actions of formal religious institutions or groups. There may be a diffusion of religious values in a society that could have peace-prone consequences even in the absence of formal actions by church bodies. For example, some analysts have argued that the wide diffusion of Christian values played a mediating role in the process that ended the apartheid regime in South Africa, even though the churches were mostly polarized between the two sides of the conflict, at least until the last few years of the regime, when the Dutch Reformed Church reversed its position on apartheid.

■ Third, *economic development.* The basic text on the relation of religion and economic development is, of course, the German sociologist Max Weber's 1905 work *The Protestant Ethic and the Spirit of Capitalism.* Scholars have been arguing over the thesis of this book for over ninety years. However one comes out on this (I happen to be an unreconstructed Weberian), it is clear that some values foster modern economic development more than others. Something *like* Weber's "Protestant ethic" is probably functional in an early phase of capitalist growth—an ethic, whether religiously inspired or not, that values personal discipline, hard work, frugality, and a respect for learning. The new Evangelicalism in Latin America exhibits these values in virtually crystalline purity, so that my own mental subtitle for the research project on this topic conducted by the center I direct at Boston University has been, "Max Weber is alive and well and living in Guatemala." Conversely, Iberian Catholicism, as it was established in Latin America, clearly does *not* foster such values.

But religious traditions can change. Spain experienced a remarkably successful period of economic development beginning in the waning years of the Franco regime, and one of the important factors was the influence of Opus Dei, which combined rigorous theological orthodoxy with a market-friendly openness in economic matters. I have suggested that Islam, by and large, has difficulties with a modern market economy; yet Muslim emigrants have done remarkably well in a number of countries (for instance, in sub-Saharan Africa), and there is a powerful Islamic movement in Indonesia that might yet play a role analogous to that of Opus Dei in the Catholic world. I should add that for years now there has been an extended debate over the part played by Confucian-inspired values in the economic success stories of East Asia; if one is to credit the "post-Confucian thesis" and also to allow that Confucianism is a religion, then here would be a very important religious contribution to economic development.

One morally troubling aspect of this matter is that values functional at one period of economic development may not be functional at another. The values of the "Protestant ethic" or a functional equivalent thereof are probably essential during the phase that Walt Rostow called "the take-off," but may not be so in a later phase. Much less austere values may be more functional in the so-called post-industrial economies of Europe, North America, and East Asia. For example, frugality, however admirable from a moral viewpoint, may actually be a vice economically speaking. Although undisciplined hedonists have a hard time climbing out of primitive poverty, they can do well in the high-tech, knowledge-driven economies of the advanced societies.

▪ Finally, *human rights and social justice.* Religious institutions have, of course, made many statements on human rights and social justice. Some of these have had important political consequences, as in the civil-rights struggle in the United States and the collapse of Communist regimes in Europe. But, as mentioned previously, there are different religiously articulated views about the nature of human rights. The same goes for ideas about social justice: what is justice to some groups is gross injustice to others. Sometimes it is very clear that positions taken by religious groups on such matters are based on a religious rationale; the principled opposition to abortion and contraception by the Roman Catholic Church is such a clear case. At other times, though, positions on social justice, even if legitimated by religious rhetoric, reflect the location of the religious functionaries in this or that network of non-religious social classes and interests. To stay with the same example, I think that this is the case with most of the positions taken by American Catholic institutions on social-justice issues other than those relating to sexuality and reproduction.

I have dealt very briefly with immensely complex matters. I was asked to give a global overview, and that is what I have tried to do. There is no way that I can end this with some sort of uplifting sermon. Both those who have great hopes for the role of religion in the affairs of this world and those who *fear* this role must be disappointed by the factual evidence. In assessing this role, there is no alternative to a nuanced, case-by-case approach. But one statement can be made with great confidence: Those who neglect religion in their analyses of contemporary affairs do so at great peril.

2

Roman Catholicism in the Age of John Paul II

George Weigel

On the edge of the twenty-first century, the impact of the Roman Catholic Church on world affairs vividly illustrates what Professor Peter Berger described in the previous chapter as the non-secularization of late modernity. That Catholic impact, which can be measured empirically from Manila to Kraków, and from Santiago de Chile to Seoul, also refutes the expectations—indeed, the deeply cherished hopes—of many of the founding fathers of the modern world.

Voltaire, it will be remembered, died with the wish that the last king be strangled with the guts of the last priest, and the revolution he helped to inspire defined its goal as little less than the overthrow of the civilization the Church had helped nurture for centuries. When Italian troops occupied Rome in 1870, completed the unification of Italy by absorbing the Papal States, and sent the pope into internal exile as the "prisoner of the Vatican," it was widely thought that the Catholic Church was a spent historical force. As recently as 1919,

George Weigel, president of the Ethics and Public Policy Center from 1989 to mid-1996, is now a senior fellow at the Center. He has written or edited sixteen books. The most recent, *Witness to Hope: The Biography of Pope John Paul II*, will be published worldwide in the fall of 1999.

only twenty-six states, mainly from Latin America, maintained diplomatic representation at the Holy See, and the Vatican was blocked (by Clause 15 of the secret accord that bound Italy to the Allies in 1915) from participating in the Versailles Peace Conference.

The view today is rather different. Roman Catholicism is now a vastly complex religious community of one billion adherents, more than 17 per cent of the world's population, living in virtually every country on the planet. Its membership shows a dazzling diversity: Helmut Kohl and Jacques Chirac, Henry Hyde and Daniel Patrick Moynihan, Mel Gibson and Martin Sheen, Mother Theresa and Lech Wałęsa, Princess Michael of Kent and Cherie (Mrs. Tony) Blair, New York Yankees manager Joe Torre and New York philanthropist Lew Lehrman, composer Henryk Górecki and "Cranberries" lead singer Dolores O'Riordan. That community of faith, worship, and charity is served by some 4,300 bishops, 404,500 priests, 848,500 women religious, and 428,000 mission catechists, who are organized into 2,842 dioceses located in venues as various as New York City, São Salvador di Bahia, Samoa-Apia, Paris, Prague, Bombay, and Kinshasa. The Church sponsors some 172,800 educational institutions around the world (running the gamut from simple village preschools to distinguished research universities) and operates some 105,100 social-welfare institutions—hospitals, dispensaries, and clinics, homes for the old, ill, and handicapped, orphanages, nurseries, and marriage counseling centers. In Third World settings, those institutions are sometimes a region's sole lifeline to modern education and medicine.

Today, 166 states exchange full diplomatic representation with the Holy See, a unique entity recognized in international law as the juridical embodiment of the universal ministry of the Bishop of Rome as the head of the Roman Catholic Church. In addition to these bilateral relations, the Holy See participates in the work of the United Nations, both in New York and in the functional U.N. agencies in Geneva and elsewhere. The Holy See also maintains diplomatic representation at regional organizations like the Organization on Security and Cooperation in Europe and the Organization of American States. Holy See representatives have served in recent years as mediators of border disputes (notably in securing the Beagle Channel boundary agreement between Chile and Argentina); and under Vatican influence, Catholic lay movements like the Rome-based Sant' Egidio Community have played important roles in "third-track diplomacy," most successfully in Mozambique. In addition, the Holy See enters into treaties (known as "concordats") with sovereign states, in order to regulate the religious, educational, and charitable activities of the Church in individual countries, and is a signatory of such international agreements as the Nuclear Non-Proliferation Treaty and the Nuclear Test-Ban Treaty. No one, of course, worried that the colorfully clad Swiss Guards who maintain security at the entrances to the 109-acre Vatican compound in Rome might test or acquire nuclear weapons; but the Holy See's participation in such international legal instruments is empirical testimony to the distinctive place it occupies in the formal, legal aspects of international public life, and to the permanence of moral issues in world politics.

Furthermore, it is now widely recognized that the Catholic Church in general, and Pope John Paul II in particular, played indispensable roles in what we have come to know as the Revolution of 1989 in east central Europe. The terms in which the Pope and the Church helped to bring about the demise of European Communism remain controverted. But that John Paul II was a key figure, and perhaps *the* key figure, in the drama of the 1980s is now conceded by Mikhail Gorbachev and Carl Bernstein, if not by the editors of the *New York Times* and *Foreign Affairs*. In a similar vein, and within roughly the same time-frame, one could also note the role played by Catholic clergy, religious, and lay leaders in the non-violent resistance to the Pinochet regime in Chile, in various other democratic transitions in Central and South America, in the overthrow of the Marcos regime in the Philippines, and in the democratization of South Korea. Voltaire must be spinning in his grave.

The Carrier of a Proposal

Interesting as all that may be, however, it is not these diplomatic and political aspects of the presence of Roman Catholicism in world affairs that are my subject here. Rather, I want to discuss Roman Catholicism as a religious community that is carrying into the twenty-first century a distinctive set of proposals for the right-ordering of societies and indeed of international life.

The century now drawing to a close has borne ample witness—often in oceans of blood, sometimes in magnificent human achievement—to Richard Weaver's maxim that "ideas have consequences." Indeed, when we think of Lenin, Churchill, Hitler, Gandhi, Nasser, Weizmann, Havel, and the Fabian professorate at the London School of Economics in the 1920 and 1930s, it seems as if the twentieth century has been singularly a time of great political ideas locked in mortal conflict. The times are, of course, achangin'. And it may well be that the world—or at least the West—is breaking free from its two-hundred-year enthrallment to politics as the principal arena of human energy and creativity and the primary determinant of history. I, for one, hope that is the case.

But suppose, for the sake of the argument, that my friend Francis Fukuyama is right and that the once bitterly contested structural questions about the organization of modern societies have been essentially settled in favor of democratic polities and market-centered economies. One would still be left (as Fukuyama himself has argued) with the great questions of culture: those habits of the mind and habits of the heart essential for channeling and disciplining the enormous energies set loose by free politics and the free economy so that they serve the ends of genuine human flourishing. Culture is crucial to keeping free societies free. And the heart of culture is "cult"—religion.

Roman Catholicism is, first and foremost, a religious community that makes certain truth claims about the human person, human community, human history, and human destiny, all understood in their relationship to God. To proclaim those truths, and to witness to them in worship and through service to humanity, is the Church's reason for existence. The Church damages its proclamation and its witness when it proposes itself as an authoritative mentor in spheres beyond its singular competence.

At the same time, however, these truths about the human person and human community are truths with *public* consequences. In developing what we refer to as Catholic social doctrine, the teaching authority of the Church and the Church's social ethicists have been drawing out those public consequences for more than a century now. Thus Roman Catholicism enters the new millennium as the bearer of a richly textured, philosophically sophisticated, and (if the term may be used neutrally of a religious community) worldly-wise set of ideas about how to create and sustain free societies and how to maintain an international public order in which freedom is at the service of peace and social justice.

That assertion may surprise those who still think Catholicism is inextricably attached to pre-modernity. Yet the truth of the matter is that the Roman Catholic critique of contemporary society is now conducted from firmly within modern culture. To be sure, there are still Roman Catholics throughout the world who yearn for an intellectual-cultural "rollback" that would repeal the Cartesian revolution and revive the simple naïveté of pre-modern consciousness. But these are fringe figures. With the Second Vatican Council (1962-1965) and the pontificate of John Paul II, Roman Catholicism has been fully inserted into the distinctively modern quest for meaning and value, for freedom, abundance, and social justice. In that process, Catholicism has learned from modernity. But now, I would argue, Roman Catholicism has important things to teach late modernity (or postmodernity, or whatever it is we imagine ourselves inhabiting in the decades ahead). And the things it has to teach are critically important for what is perhaps *the* great public question of twenty-first-century life, domestically and internationally: the question of the responsible use of human freedom.

The Radical Pope

We cannot get a fix on Roman Catholicism in the next century without taking the measure of the papacy of John Paul II: a pontificate of greater intellectual significance for the Church and its address to the world than any other since the Reformation, in my judgment.

This is not a simple task, for John Paul II is both a deeply convinced Christian believer and a complex, subtle intellectual—a combination that for many in the American opinion-merchandising industry is a contradiction in terms. When you add to those qualities of spirit and intellect the Pope's demonstrable political skills, the result is a large-scale figure of the sort we are not accustomed to seeing in recent years. It was no papal apologist but rather the thoroughly secular and left-leaning London *Independent* that described John Paul II in early 1995 as "the only truly global leader left" at the end of the twentieth century.

This is not the place to delve deeply into John Paul II's intellectual project, which has evolved over the past fifty years in conversation with the work of such modern intellectual giants as Edmund Husserl and Max Scheler, Paul Ricoeur, Emmanuel Levinas, and Leszek Kołakowski. Suffice it to say, by way of background, that Karol Wojtyła is the first pope in history, not only to have had a modern intellectual formation, but to have been a creative figure in European intellectual life prior to his election to the papacy. Indeed, no pope since Benedict XIV (1740-1758) has maintained during his papacy such a wide array of active intellectual contacts—including biennial seminars at the papal summer residence for philosophers (many of them agnostic or atheist) and hard scientists (ditto).

In his 1994 bestseller *Crossing the Threshold of Hope,* the Pope gave millions of readers some glimpses into his distinctive philosophical position. He understands that the Cartesian "turn to the subject" is an irremovable reference point for philosophy today; but he is convinced that modern subjectivism can easily decompose into a solipsism that degrades both individuals and civil society. John Paul II has a phenomenologist's appreciation of the infinite complexity of human moral action; but he is also convinced that there are moral absolutes that individuals and societies ignore at their peril. He has the true intellectual's commitment to a deepening of knowledge through open dialogue, or what he has termed the "method of persuasion"; yet he is also convinced that there are unchangeable truths to be known about the human condition, and that these have public as well as personal consequences.

As pope, Karol Wojtyła does not function as an authoritarian ruler, imposing his personal philosophical and theological convictions on a community by virtue of the power of his office. Rather, in the Catholic understanding of that office, Wojtyła is the servant and custodian of an *authoritative* religious and moral tradition, a tradition that, in its public moral aspects, proposes itself as a body of truths that can be grasped by all people of good will. To the nurturance and proclamation of that tradition he brings, of course, whatever gifts of intellect he has. Thus there has been, in the pontificate of John Paul II, a significant development of Catholic social doctrine, influenced by the Pope's pre-papal philosophical work, his experience of totalitarianism, his encounters with the democratic world, and his pastoral concern for the Third World, in which well over half of the world's Roman Catholics now live.

The point to be underscored, though, is that the social doctrine of Roman Catholicism is not "for Catholics only." When he addresses the worlds of international politics and economics, John Paul II, like his predecessors in the tradition of Catholic social doctrine dating back to Pope Leo XIII in the late nineteenth century, understands himself to be articulating *public,* not sectarian, truths. And he asks the world to consider those truths on their own merits, irrespective of its beliefs about the office in which he serves.

The Universality of Human Rights

This interaction between the public moral claims of Catholic social doctrine (as recently developed by John Paul II) and controverted issues in world politics came into sharp focus during the Pope's address to the United Nations on October 6, 1995.

This was the Holy Father's second appearance at the U.N. The first had taken place in October 1979, not quite a year after his election as the first Slavic pontiff in history and the first non-Italian pope in 455 years. In the media haze surrounding "John Paul Superstar" (as *Time* dubbed him in 1979), insufficient attention may have been paid to the substance of that 1979 U.N. address, which was a forthright defense of basic human rights as the moral foundation of any just polity and of any international order capable of fostering peace among nations. In the course of that address, the Pope paid particular attention to the fundamental right of religious freedom for all peoples—the first of human rights, in John Paul II's catechism.[1] As events in east central Europe would shortly illustrate, this papal stress on the centrality of religious freedom could have powerful political consequences.

The Pope's 1995 U.N. address came six years after the Revolution of 1989 seemed to have proven the trans-cultural moral power of human-rights claims and the political potency of dedicated, often religiously motivated human-rights movements. Yet in the wake of the Communist crackup in central and eastern Europe, new voices had been raised, once again challenging the very notion of the "universality" of human rights. East Asian autocrats proclaimed a "Confucian way" in which basic immunities of the person from coercive state power were subordinated to the demands of public order—as defined by authorities who declined to subject their custody of public order to public scrutiny. At the Vienna World Conference on Human Rights in June 1993, these same autocrats were joined by certain militant Islamicists in denouncing the moral claims embedded in the 1948 Universal Declaration of Human Rights as examples of "Western imperialism." Meanwhile, in Western Europe and North America, postmodernist and deconstructionist theorists were arguing, in contemporary variations on Jeremy Bentham, that the very idea of human rights was "nonsense on stilts," because there is no universal human nature about which such rights could be asserted.

John Paul II argued that this new assault on universality posed a serious danger to the consolidation of humanity's hard-won victories over the various totalitarianisms of our bloody century. These victories were not, the Pope suggested, to be understood in narrow ethnic, national, ideological, or religious terms. Rather, the victory over Fascism and Communism had been a triumph of the human spirit, which had asserted its thirst for freedom across virtually the entire range of the world's cultures. Thus the Pope began his U.N. address by underlining the *global* character of the world human-rights revolution:

> On the threshold of a new millennium we are witnessing an extraordinary global acceleration of that quest for freedom which is one of the great dynamics of human history. This phenomenon is not limited to any one part of the world nor is it the expression of any single culture. Men and women throughout the world, even when threatened by violence, have taken the risk of freedom, asking to be given a place in social, political, and economic life that is commensurate with their dignity as free human beings. This universal longing for freedom is truly one of the distinguishing marks of our time.[2]

But, the Pope continued, this revolution of rising political expectations should not be understood simply in terms of a demand for changing the structures of public life when those structures repress human freedom and creativity, important as such changes were, and are. The world human-rights revolution also had an "inner structure," a common *moral* core that could be discerned amidst the vast diversity of the world's cultures. And that moral reality was a fact with enormous public consequences:

> It is important for us to grasp what might be called the inner structure of this world-wide movement. It is precisely its global character which offers us its first and fundamental "key" and confirms that there are indeed universal human rights rooted in the nature of the person, rights which reflect the objective and inviolable demands of a universal moral law. These are not abstract points; rather, these rights tell us something about the actual life of every individual and of every social group. They also remind us that we do not live in an irrational or meaningless world. On the contrary, there is a moral logic which is built into human life and which makes possible dialogue between individuals and peoples. If we want a century of violent coercion to be succeeded by a century of persuasion, we must find a way to discuss the human future intelligibly. The universal moral law written on the human heart is precisely that kind of "grammar" which is needed if the world is to engage this discussion of its future.[3]

The attack on the universality of human rights was troubling not only in its potential impact on individuals but also because it involved a denial of the very possibility of an international politics, if politics be understood in the classical sense as mutual deliberation about the common good:

> To be sure, there is no single model for organizing the politics and economics of human freedom; different cultures and different historical experiences give rise to different institutional forms of public life in a free and responsible society. But it is one thing to affirm a legitimate pluralism of "forms of freedom" and another to deny any universality or intelligibility to the nature of man or to the human experience. The latter makes the international politics of persuasion extremely difficult, if not impossible.[4]

Note that, in defending the universality of human rights, John Paul II was making not univocally Catholic claims but moral claims that he thought could be engaged by every rational person. Moreover, the Pope's philosophical defense of the universality of human rights, in which he proclaimed once again the "first right" of religious freedom, was a defense of the very possibility of an international order, and especially one characterized more by persuasion than by violent coercion. If there are no universal human rights, the Pope argued, that must mean there is no universal human nature. And if there is no universal human nature from which men and women can "read" certain moral norms that can structure a reasonable conversation about the world's future, then there will be no such conversation, and coercion will inevitably follow.

Parenthetically, it is in this public moral context—the defense of the universality of human rights—that we should understand the Holy See's vigorous intervention at the September 1994 World Conference on Population and Development, held in Cairo. Contrary to the complaints of U.N. population-control bureaucrats, the U.S. Undersecretary of State for Global Affairs, and many of the Western media, John Paul II's resistance to the establishment of an internationally recognized right to abortion-on-demand was not a matter of imposing a peculiar Catholic moral crotchet on a pluralistic world. Rather, the Pope was defending what he believes is a fundamental and inalienable human right, whose protection in law is indispensable to the sustaining of free societies: the right to life from conception until natural death. The Catholic argument at Cairo was made in explicitly *public* terms, as demonstrated by the fact that it garnered support from a wide range of states. Indeed, if there was any effort at "imposition" going on at Cairo, it was the effort to impose the morals of the Western sexual revolution on the world through international law, multilateral and bilateral foreign aid, and coercive state power.

Development of a Social Doctrine

The mainstream of Roman Catholic political philosophy has insisted, at least since St. Augustine, that politics, even international politics, has an irreducible moral content. For politics is a human activity, and human action—as the expression of human intelligence and free will—is moral action. This tradition has been further refined, with an eye toward the twenty-first century, by John Paul II's reflections on the moral structure of the politics of freedom.

It was a mere two years after the Communist crackup that the Pope asked (in so many words) whether the crisis of Communism might not be followed in short order by the crisis of democracy. The root of the Communist failure, he argued in the 1991 encyclical *Centesimus Annus,* lay in Communism's false anthropology, its desperately defective understanding of the human person. Might a similarly defective anthropology—in this case, utilitarian/pragmatic rather than Marxist-Leninist—create a crisis for the seemingly triumphant democracies? The experience of the human-rights resistance in east central Europe during the 1980s the "power of the powerless," as Václav Havel dubbed it—seemed to have demonstrated that a robust civil society was both an antidote to tyranny and a precondition to healthy democracy. But could a robust civil society be built on a foundation of principled moral skepticism? Here is John Paul II in what became perhaps the most controversial paragraph of *Centesimus Annus:*

> Nowadays there is a tendency to claim that agnosticism and skeptical relativism are the philosophy and the basic attitude which correspond to democratic forms of political life. . . . It must be observed in this regard that if there is no ultimate truth to guide and direct political activity, then ideas and convictions can easily be manipulated for reasons of power. As history demonstrates, a democracy without values easily turns into open or thinly disguised totalitarianism. [#46]

To put it in more graphic historical terms, and with apologies to Marx and Engels, a specter is haunting the democracies: the specter of Weimar. Inter-war Germany had a most elegantly crafted constitution, one of whose principal architects was the great sociologist Max Weber. But Weimar Germany lacked the habits of mind and heart—the public moral culture—necessary to sustain democratic self-governance, and the results were catastrophic. The lesson would seem to be clear: the civil society necessary to sustain democracy cannot be constructed out of an infinite series of pragmatic bargains. Unless freedom is tethered to certain basic truths about human beings, freedom becomes its own undoing, as liberty becomes mere license and politics descends into Hobbes's war of all against all.

In the 1993 encyclical *Veritatis Splendor,* John Paul II further developed this proposal for the moral buttressing of the free and virtuous society. How, he asked, can free societies sustain their commitment to the bedrock democratic principle of equality before the law? Human beings are clearly unequal in intelligence, physical capability, and beauty. Given the fact of inequality, how can men and women build and sustain a free society in which the radical equality of all before the law is a constituting political-philosophical principle? Only, John Paul II argues, by recognizing that our fundamental equality as citizens rests on our fundamental equality before the moral law, a set of moral norms that is hard-wired into human beings as an essential constituent of our humanity (a point the Pope reiterated at the U.N. in 1995).[5]

Ethnic, religious, racial, and cultural differences are among the defining characteristics of contemporary societies on this rapidly shrinking planet; communities of civic friendship that bridge those differences are essential to the civil society that makes democracy possible. How can plurality be transformed into community without emptying distinctive cultures of their content? Only, John Paul claims, if "social coexistence" is based on "a morality which acknowledges certain norms as valid always and for everyone, with no exception."[6]

How can democracies promote and defend integrity in public life? The problem, the Pope suggests, cannot be resolved by a constant thickening of government ethics manuals, but only by a broad cultural acknowledgment of certain moral truths about the dignity of the human person.[7]

How can democracies foster those habits of self-discipline and self-command by which their citizens avoid entrapment in what Zbigniew Brezinski has termed the "permissive cornucopia"? Only, John Paul argues, by fostering a robust public moral culture that recognizes the universality of certain basic norms of decency, which in turn reflect essential truths about the nature of the human person.

The free society, in other words, is not simply a matter of its political and economic institutions. The free society is an ongoing experiment in a people's capacity for self-governance. The health of the free society and its political and economic institutions is dependent on the vitality of its public moral culture.

It will probably strike some as an exercise in *chutzpah* for the leader of a church that had once looked upon democracy with extreme skepticism—if not downright hostility—to presume to define for democracies the moral conditions required for their continued existence. But John Paul's social doctrine cannot be rightly understood as mere papal scolding. His theory of democracy does include a sharp challenge to the skeptical relativism that is currently fashionable in American high culture and in American philosophy departments. But here the Pope is in company with thinkers and commentators as diverse as Michael Sandel and Robert Bork in arguing that the "procedural republic"—which removes all moral reference points from our common life on the radically relativistic grounds that a democracy cannot adjudicate between competing moral systems—is an illusion that will ultimately prove self-destructive.

Moreover, I would suggest that the Pope's call for a reconsideration of the intrinsic relationship between freedom and truth is first and foremost an expression of his humanism: his basic convictions about the inalienable dignity of human beings, who are never mere individuals but are *persons* endowed with intelligence and free will, and thus with the capacity for moral reason and moral choice.

In the contemporary Catholic view of things, as articulated by John Paul II, democracy is the system of government that most coheres with human dignity because democracy allows for the public exercise of moral responsibility by free human persons, who always concretize their freedom in communities—familial, religious, ethnic, civic, political. The free or market-oriented economy is the economic system that best coheres with human dignity because it creates scope for the exercise of human creativity and allows for the free participation of free persons in the circle of productivity and exchange. But neither democracy nor the market is a machine that will run by itself, according to John Paul II. The free society has three components: a democratic polity, a free economy, and a vibrant public moral culture. And it is the robustness of the latter, the public moral culture, that is the key to the proper functioning of the politics and economics of freedom.

A Post-Constantinian Model?

This intense focus on culture as the key to the flourishing of free societies in the twenty-first century marks a development in the Catholic Church's approach to public affairs. In the first thirty years of the post–World War II period, the Holy See's vigorous re-entry into international public life took place in classic "high-politics" terms: bilateral negotiations and agreements with sovereign states, and participation in international organizations, amplified by the occasional moral exhortation, usually couched in rather abstract terms. That bilateral and multilateral international engagement continues, as we have seen. But the diplomacy of the Holy See now takes place within a new context set by John Paul II's global defense of basic human rights for all peoples, which is in itself a statement about the priority of culture over politics and economics.

Moreover, John Paul II has been remarkably unhesitant to challenge the powers that be, in states or in international organizations. But he has done so, not in the style of a Renaissance prince demanding certain institutional prerogatives for the Church, but as a witness to what he believes are fundamental moral truths about human beings. And when this has required a confrontation with what an older generation would have called the "principalities and powers" of this age, John Paul II has not hesitated to speak truth to power, thereby defying certain of the protocols of diplomatic behavior that his immediate predecessors had typically observed.

If by the "Constantinian Church" we mean a church that was fully participant in public life but that tended to accept many of the canons of public life as "the world" defined them, it might be argued that John Paul II has been developing a "post-Constantinian" model for twenty-first-century Catholicism. This is emphatically not a church bent on returning to the pre-Constantinian catacombs. But it is a church that, having passed through a lengthy Constantinian phase, has reacquired a certain critical distance from the worlds of power, precisely in order to help hold those worlds accountable to universal moral norms.

Viewed from one angle, this post-Constantinian Church will be less of a "threat" to politics, in that the Church no longer seeks, and in fact flatly rejects, the mantle of coercive state power as a buttress to its evangelical mission. But it will, from another angle, be a dangerous church, for it will carry into public life an understanding of "politics" that is far more morally charged than most established democracies seem to find comfortable these days.

The development of this new model of Catholic engagement with public life has not been even across the full range of pressing issues in world politics today. While the official Church seems to have found a vocabulary for arguing its case for religious freedom and other basic human rights, it has been less successful in articulating a moral framework for making judgments about the legitimate use of armed force in the defense of freedom and justice. The Pope, for example, has spoken of the *duty* of humanitarian intervention in cases of genocide; but neither he nor any other Vatican official has specified on whom that duty rests, or how the classic criteria of the just-war tradition bear on the understanding of how that duty might be fulfilled.

It is curious that so intellectually assertive a pontificate as John Paul II's has not sought to foster a development of the just-war tradition to meet the exigencies of the contemporary political and military situation. For the questions that history is pressing on moral theorists, statesmen, and military leaders today are both unprecedented and urgent. Is pre-emptive military action legitimate against rogue regimes threatening the use of weapons of mass destruction? Is strategic defense against the use of such weapons by rogue regimes with ballistic-missile capability a moral imperative? How is the just-war tradition, which was designed to regulate international public life in a world of sovereign states, to address the serious moral problems for world politics posed by non-state actors—ranging from financial institutions to terrorist organizations—today? What level of political authority (which is inescapably moral authority) are we to invest in that often-cited but vaguely defined phenomenon, "the international community"? And where is the authority of this "community" lodged: in international organizations, coalitions of states, regional security organizations? By whose authority is "humanitarian intervention" through military force conducted? These are some of the fascinating—and politically urgent—questions left unattended to date by the pontificate of this most internationally visible pope.

One might also regard the Holy See's continued investment of enormous energies in the United Nations and its functional agencies, which are hardly paragons of morally serious political institutions, as a curious hangover from the "Constantinian" Church. That the Church has not articulated a critique of the moral, financial, and political corruption of the U.N. system that even remotely resembles in intensity the critique that the Pope has brought to bear on individual states is, to put it gently, something of an anomaly.

Still, if the great public question of the twenty-first century will be the responsible use of a human freedom to which technology will give ever-widening scope, then what the Holy See's Permanent Representative to the U.N. does or does not say about the inadequacies of that institution matters far less than what John Paul II has said, preached, and written about the intrinsic relationship between freedom and truth. The degree to which that teaching has been internalized by one billion Catholics around the world varies widely, of course; truth to tell, it varies within the College of Cardinals and the Roman Curia. But if ideas indeed have consequences, then it is surely consequential that an ancient religious tradition has gathered itself to advance a proposal for securing the future of free societies that speaks to some of the most deeply controverted questions of the age.

It is also worth noting, in the context of this volume, that Roman Catholicism seems far more capable, today, of making genuinely public moral arguments about the right-ordering of societies and the conduct of international public life than any other world religious body. Without abandoning its distinctive theological commitments, the Catholic Church has, over the past thirty-five years, developed a capacity to foster an international public moral argument in which those who do not share Catholic theological convictions can participate fully. If the twenty-first century is going to be an age of culturally assertive religion—and if that fact of life is going to result in a deepening and broadening of the world's conversation about the world's future, rather than in chaos and sectarian strife—then the capacity to build a genuine pluralism out of religious plurality is going to loom increasingly large.

Plura*lism* doesn't simply happen. Genuine *pluralism* is built out of plurality when differences are debated rather than ignored and a unity begins to be discerned in human affairs—what John Courtney Murray called "the unity of an orderly conversation." Nor is the achievement of pluralism a matter of ongoing pragmatic bargaining. Commitments to the "method of persuasion" in politics as well as in intellectual life require sturdier warrants than utilitarian accommodation.

Thus the paradox of the situation, at least insofar as the world imagines paradoxes, is that it is precisely the depth of the Catholic commitment to the Church's theologically grounded understanding of certain basic moral truths about the human person that secures the Church's commitment to the "method of persuasion" in both evangelization and politics. The more deeply "Catholic" the Church becomes, the more robustly committed it will be to the achievement of a genuine pluralism in the world.

This may be something of a genuine *novum* in history. Culturally assertive religion has, for the past five thousand years, tended to be politically aggressive religion, in the sense that self-confident religious communities have frequently sought to put political (and military) power behind their theological claims. Roman Catholicism has certainly been susceptible to this temptation over the course of its two-thousand-year history.

But now, on the cusp of a new millennium, Catholicism has developed a serious theological rationale for rejecting the use of coercive state power in the service of religious truth, and for fostering a broad-gauged public conversation about the "oughts" of our common life, within and among nations, amidst a wide diversity of religious, philosophical, and cultural viewpoints. Given the kind of world our children and grandchildren are likely to inherit—a rapidly shrinking, thoroughly non-secularized world, in which intense religious convictions and passions will constantly intersect with the worlds of politics and economics—that development is not of interest only to Roman Catholics. The model of religious engagement it can provide, and the examples of such engagement that this model will generate, are of utmost importance for the future of world affairs.

3

The Evangelical Upsurge and
Its Political Implications

David Martin

For the last three or four decades there has been a steady global upsurge in conservative Protestant Christianity parallel to the upsurge in conservative Islam. Indeed, these have been the two main shifts in world religion during the second half of the twentieth century. The advance of conservative Evangelicalism has been most evident in what used to be called the Third World, especially Latin America and sub-Saharan Africa, but it is also notable in the Philippines, the Pacific rim (above all Korea), and China. Sizable conversions have occurred in parts of Eastern Europe, notably Romania. And Evangelical religion can clearly claim to be the liveliest sector in the developed "Western" world, whether we speak of Britain, Holland, the United States, or Australia.

Just what the overall numbers are is difficult to say, partly because numbers are propaganda, but also because there are varying criteria for what constitutes affiliation and because there is a penumbra of

David Martin is emeritus professor of sociology at the London School of Economics, a visiting professor at Lancaster University, and an international associate of the Institute for the Study of Economic Culture, Boston University. Among the books he has written are *Tongues of Fire: Conservative Protestantism in Latin America* and *A General Theory of Secularization*.

fringe movements. Most estimates of Evangelicals in Latin America hover between forty and fifty million, which is about one person in ten. The total in Africa must also be in the tens of millions, and optimistic estimates are similar for China. Maybe in the world as a whole we are talking about 200 million people.

The problem is that the main upsurge is not in the older, more staid Evangelicalism but in Pentecostalism. That means we are dealing with movements offering what are called the "gifts of the Spirit" (such as healing, prophecy, speaking in tongues), rather than with what some people label "fundamentalism." At the same time, there are plenty of versions of the older mainstream churches "in renewal," which represent a spill-over of the Pentecostal spirit. Alongside them are myriads of small churches, many of them quite local, as well as charismatic fellowships. And there are also thriving mega-churches, often with a neo-Pentecostal emphasis on health and wealth. Indeed, health-and-wealth churches seem to resonate very easily with the emphases of traditional African religion. There are, finally, syncretistic movements at the margin of evangelical Christianity, such as the Universal Church of the Kingdom of God, in Brazil, and The Light of the World, in Mexico, each with about two million followers.

It is important to note the missionary provenance of this momentous shift in world religious affairs. Initially there was a tendency to pigeonhole Evangelical expansion as a form of American cultural imperialism, supported by American money and spearheaded by American missionary personnel, including the televangelists. However, most recent research recognizes that, whatever the origins of some of these movements in the North Atlantic Protestant world, they are now independent and indigenous in both personnel and finance. In the contemporary world of mass communications and geographical mobility, the missionary is no longer necessary. Missionaries exist, of course, but even if they did not the Evangelical expansion would be much the same, given the capacity of religious messages to pass along lines of personal and familial contact. People and ideas are on the move at increasing speeds.

TRAITS AFFECTING POLITICAL IMPACT

Certain characteristics of Evangelical and especially of Pentecostal religion bear upon the likely character of any substantial political presence. Crucially, Evangelicals and Pentecostals have carried forward traditions of the separation of church and state. Also, they are so fragmented that they cannot hope to operate in concert to establish some kind of ideological monopoly. In that respect they are quite unlike "fundamentalist" Muslims, who in many countries seek ideological hegemony and the regulation of all citizens according to Islamic law. Evangelical Christians are, with one or two exceptions, ambitious at most to constitute an effective pressure group, pressing corporate institutional interests and broad moral principles, and generally acquiring a voice in the public forum.

Another characteristic likely to affect the form that Evangelicals' intervention and influence takes is their considerable suspicion of "the world," expressed through a concentration on building up the body of the faithful as a separated enclave of righteousness. Thus the initial impact of Evangelical conversion occurs not through overt political action but as a major mutation of culture: restoration of the family, the rejection of *machismo,* the adoption of economic and work disciplines and new priorities. Occasionally this phase of cultural accumulation and the establishment of autonomous space may issue in more direct political action, as it did in the black civil-rights movement in the United States and, for an earlier example, in the association of British Nonconformists with the Liberal Party 1870-1920.

But these rather dramatic excursions are exceptional. As I said above, the more usual mode of political intervention has to do with establishing a voice that expresses both the institutional interests of what has become a substantial sector of the world of voluntary association and a concern for broad moral principles. This voice may make itself heard through negotiations with local authorities, or through candidacies within established parties. Beyond that, the Evangelical presence is felt through the large number able to vote for the candidates or parties most sympathetic to the Evangelical point of view.

Individualism and Pragmatism

The Evangelical understanding of the political realm, when not suffused with suspicion, tends to be at once individualistic and pragmatic and thus to correspond to historical features of political life in Anglo-Saxon democracies. Its individualistic approach supposes that political improvement depends on the multiplication of persons of moral integrity; the preferred discourse is through personalized images rather than structural arrangements and forces. And its pragmatism ensures that Evangelicals are resistant to political doctrine and the language of "project" that pervades Latin European and Latin American political discussion. At the most there is a strain towards neo-liberal positions and a rejection of kinds of socialism that express the anti-religious traditions of the Enlightenment. In Latin America the Evangelical and Pentecostal experience of the comprehensive world-views of Marxism and Catholicism (or the two combined) has not been positive, and that is expressed in voting behavior.

Obviously there are contrasts here with both Islamic and Catholic interventions. In contrast with Islam, there is no body of legal norms to promote as the basis for an Evangelical society. While some minor currents of Evangelical opinion advocate a reorganization of society along Levitical lines, these currents are not influential and are highly unlikely to acquire serious influence in Latin America. In contrast with Catholicism, there are no historic norms worked out over centuries of experience of power and politics to draw upon. As Evangelicals experience the intricate dynamics of the political sphere, they have no traditions to use as guides. What they have instead, at least in Latin America, are the established practices of corporatism and clientage, and it is all too easy to adjust to these practices. As a result, the traditional Evangelical fears of the corruption that can follow from dealings with the "principalities and powers" have occasionally proved well founded.

In the absence of sophisticated norms deployed by high-status ecclesiastics and religious intellectuals, Evangelicals are exposed to the vagaries of circumstance equipped with little more than native good sense and the limited inferences they can draw from the Bible. They lack markers to stabilize their responses. At the same time they are not misled, as some Catholics seem to be, into supposing that the existence of such markers means that popular piety is aware of them and can be mobilized behind them. Whether one is thinking of the analyses proposed by liberation theologians such as Leonardo Boff and Gustavo Gutiérrez or the reflections of Pope John Paul II, these are not the major influence upon the Catholic population, whose everyday practice of piety is governed by personal and local concerns. Once this is taken into account, the contrast between Evangelicals and Catholics is really not so great.

Creating a Space

Perhaps this is the point that will draw this broad introduction together. What we have initially as a consequence of the Evangelical upsurge is the creation of an autonomous social space within which people may participate in the creation of a different kind of sub-society. In this sub-society, those who count for little or nothing in the wider world find themselves addressed as persons able to display initiative and to be of consequence. Divine validation loosens their tongues, and they engage in a free communication with one another within the constraints of vigorous pastoral authority. Moreover, as these enclaves multiply, religious monopoly breaks down and pluralism develops, mediation gives way to direct access, and a competitive religious economy is established.

Taken in themselves, these features of participation, pluralism, direct access, and competition might seem to imply both democracy and the market economy. However, it is not that simple. In societies like those of Brazil and Nigeria where corruption, corporatism, and clientage are endemic, established culture exercises a centripetal pull on every kind of sub-society or resistant enclave. But in none of today's established democracies was democracy built in a day. A whole series of cooperating circumstances has to be assembled, and even then the democracy that results is always in danger of corrosion or corruption. The large-scale growth of voluntary religious associations based on participation and competition is only one rung on the ladder to the eventual establishment of a viable democracy and civil society. Nonetheless, the emergence of more and more significant social actors whose interests have to be taken into account can only help the prospects for democracy.

Two further aspects of Evangelical/Pentecostal mores enhance the democratic potential: the exercise of authority, and peaceability. Authority in Pentecostalism is concentrated in a male pastorate; in that respect the movement resembles Christianity as a whole in that it consists largely of women and is run largely by men. At the same time, many different roles and responsibilities are available, and this enables all members, male and female, to participate. It is also arguable that a movement based on spontaneous expression of "gifts of the Spirit" can survive only if there is a stable and unquestioned frame of authoritative governance. Spontaneity depends on boundaries.

As for peaceability, we have already noted the undermining of *machismo*. The male ceases to be predatory and irresponsible and becomes domesticized. In the reconstituted Evangelical family, the respect traditionally given to the male has to be earned. Moreover, males are withdrawn from the romanticism of violence. Not only are they no longer expected to respond to mayhem with mayhem, but they are emphatically not natural candidates for a Kalashnikov culture, either as guerrillas or as agents of the national security state. There is a civilian quality about the Evangelical man. Naturally this also means he may abstain from militant engagement in situations of social injustice, for example on the shop floor. But on the whole the adoption of a peaceable temper should help diminish the cycles of violence characteristic of Latin American society and the societies of sub-Saharan Africa.

EXAMPLES OF EVANGELICAL POLITICAL IMPACT

For examples of the foregoing broad principles of Evangelical impact on politics I will rely on a variety of sources, but in particular on the work of Paul Freston on Latin America.[1] I do not intend to discuss the exhaustively analyzed case of American Evangelicalism and the "Moral Majority" or "Christian Coalition" except to say that most of their particular political and moral concerns are specific to the North American context and are not extensively reproduced in other parts of the world. In Latin America, Africa, and elsewhere, the clash is not between Evangelicals or "fundamentalists" and the secular humanism of liberals in the East Coast elite; this set of issues barely arises. Furthermore, the role of televangelism is very much muted elsewhere. American Evangelicals do of course have in common with other Evangelicals concerns about matters having to do with the family and sexuality.

We will look first at three sharply contrasting cases in Latin America: Peru, Guatemala, and Brazil. In Peru the Evangelicals compose only some 7 per cent of the population and are mostly not Pentecostal. In Guatemala, Evangelicals compose some 30 per cent and are overwhelmingly Pentecostals and charismatics, but the politically significant sector involves a unique penetration of the elite by neo-Pentecostals. In Brazil, Evangelicals are about 15 per cent and the majority of them are Pentecostal, above all in the massive Assemblies of God churches; but there is an extraordinary gamut of kinds of Evangelicals, ranging from middle-class charismatics and mega-churches like "Renascer" to the lower-class "God is Love" church, which has minimal political involvement, and the Universal Church of the Kingdom of God, which is contentious and politically activist.

Evangelicalism in Latin America

The Evangelical minority in **Peru** was mobilized with other out-groups as part of "Cambio 90," the successful presidential campaign of Alberto Fujimori. The aim of Fujimori's campaign organizers was to gain access to the indigenous vote and the world of small vendors through the Evangelical network. Nineteen Protestants were elected to the congress in that 1990 election, mostly from the historical churches, and a Baptist pastor became second vice-president. After the election, however, Fujimori marginalized his support of Evangelicals and opened negotiations with the Catholic Church.

In **Guatemala**, where a long-standing civil war finally concluded in 1996, Evangelicals have become major figures in running social work and education. The two Evangelical presidents, Efraín Ríos Montt (1982-83) and Jorge Serrano (1991-93), were both members of the political class prior to their conversion to neo-Pentecostal elite metropolitan churches, Verbo and El Shaddai. This situation illustrates the penetration of a particular variant of Pentecostalism into the modern business elite, but it does not seem that Serrano's election was due in particular to the Evangelical vote among the people at large.

The **Brazil**ian case is inevitably the most significant, since it involves nearly half the southern continent. Historical Protestantism had for some time had a minor political presence, without denominational endorsement. But 1986 brought a marked increase in Protestant representation in the congress as well as a shift toward more denominational endorsement of Pentecostals, especially from the Assemblies of God. Members of this new group of representatives came from lower social origins than their predecessors and were closely associated with the Pentecostal leadership. The number of practicing Pentecostals was not so far behind the number of practicing Catholics, and the Evangelical representatives went beyond cultural defense (in issues of family and sexuality) and the promotion of their institutional interests to contest the symbolic role of the Catholic Church in the public forum. Most Evangelical representatives were on the center-right or center. As for the Evangelical electorate, though far from uniform, it probably worked against the left-wing candidate Lula in 1989 and may even have been crucial in the election of 1994. Some indications of increasing influence are the greater respect and sensitivity shown from the left and the propensity of politicians on the left to use Evangelical language, and occasionally even to convert. Paul Freston adds that an Evangelical left has emerged in Brazil. He warns against the triumphalist tendencies among some Pentecostals and what he regards as the destabilizing effects of the political interventions of the Universal Church of the Kingdom of God.[2]

Mention of the Universal Church in Brazil permits a side glance at its equally expansive and syncretic parallel in **Mexico**, The Light of the World. Only by an act of conceptual charity are these two churches categorized as Pentecostal. What is interesting about The Light of the World is that it effectively runs the district of Provincia Hermosa in Guadalajara and has done so on the basis of close relations with the Permanent Revolutionary Party (PRI). The Light of the World has a temple holding some 15,000, with an exotic atmosphere and hints of Zionism. It was founded in the thirties by a former sergeant in the Mexican civil war and shares the anti-Catholic nationalism of the PRI. At the same time it is flexible and acute enough to have also established good relations with PAN, the Catholic party, to the considerable irritation of church representatives.

In Latin American Evangelicalism as a whole, the institutional interests of the denominational leaderships are by no means always a guide to the way believers vote. Evangelicals insert themselves where they can acquire a voice. In 1974 in **Chile**, for example, the majority of denominational leaders, in common with the Catholic leadership, welcomed Pinochet, but voting behavior before and after Pinochet does not display any affinity with his regime. Evangelicals in Chile make up nearly 20 per cent of the electorate, but they do not have a single member in the legislature. The situation in **Colombia** illustrates the search for a voice as well as the promotion of institutional interests. In the election of 1990, Evangelicals emerged as an electoral entity seeking adequate civil rights, and since then small parties have also expressed the political concerns of leaders of Bogota's megachurches.

Evangelicalism in Africa

The two African countries where Evangelical influence is most likely are Nigeria and Zimbabwe. In **Nigeria** the return to democracy is still in the balance, but there are many middle-class charismatic churches that are much more politically conscious than their poorer Pentecostal brethren. These churches often represent a university-educated Christian elite that practices economic discipline, emphasizes the integrity of the family, and seeks to replace corruption by trust in public and business affairs. The problem with such a vision is that it is likely to be blunted by the high politics of patronage. In **Zimbabwe** the Assemblies of God denomination by itself accounts for something like 10 per cent of the population. Pentecostalism began in the colonial period as an anti-colonial movement, and it has since then tended to express the interests of women and young men against older male power, as well as the unassuaged traumas of the civil war. A very general point about African situations is that with the widespread collapse of state provision, the mainstream churches have operated as NGOs in association with government while Pentecostalism has come to act as a kind of opposition.

A distinctive approach that is associated in particular with Paul

Gifford assimilates Pentecostal influence in Africa into the broad category "fundamentalism."[3] In my own view, "fundamentalism" is a ragbag category joining together disparate movements: believers in biblical literalism do not necessarily accept the charismatic practice of the "gifts of the Spirit." Be that as it may, Gifford speaks in terms of an explosion of "fundamentalism"—much of it having relationships with the American South—that is eroding the influence of the mainstream Protestant churches as well as bringing about a Pentecostalization of the older bodies. He points out that a completely different dynamic from that of North America prevails in Africa. All churches, whether mainstream or independent or Pentecostal, take the Bible literally. Almost all states are opposed to abortion and are unaware of "gay rights" issues or Western-style feminism. Neither evolution nor humanism figures in discussions.

Gifford focuses on Liberia as a prime instance of a kind of Christian dualism separating church from world but with a component of health-and-wealth doctrine. Liberia is, of course, a special case, with its long-term ties to the United States (it was founded in 1822 through the efforts of an American group to settle freed American slaves in West Africa) and with the role Christianity has had in relation to the power of the Americo-Liberian oligarchy and the dominance of the True Whig party. In the latter years of William Tolbert's presidency (1971-80) the mainstream churches distanced themselves somewhat from the dominant oligarchy, and at the same time a sizable group of Christians emerged under the banner of the Evangelical Fellowship of Liberia. The Evangelical Fellowship was reacting against the close identification of mainstream Christianity with the establishment, and it adopted an apolitical stance. As in a number of Latin American churches, charismatic Christianity in Liberia carries an overtone of Christian Zionism, one implication of which is opposition to Islam.

Evangelicalism in Asia and Europe

The tendency to abjure political involvement exists elsewhere. In **Korea**, evangelical Christianity coalesces with existing cultural traits already oriented towards achievement with the result that the religious impact is largely restricted to cultural reform. It sponsors self-help and mutual insurance programs and exhibits a piety allied to technological pragmatism. As Grant Wacker put it in another context, Pentecostalism seeks out the Garden of Eden equipped with a satellite dish.[4] These traits in association with the economic and family ethos already noted are important in the reform of culture.

The **Philippines** is another country anchored historically within the U.S. sphere of influence. In 1992 a Protestant, Fidel Ramos, was elected as the country's president. In a recent volume the argument is made that the spiritual warfare embraced by Philippine charismatic groups overlaps military activity against Communism.[5] As in Guatemala, there are charismatics among the elite. Sophisticated use is made of radio, and there are extensive networks in education. There is also a margin of so-called dominion theology (from the Psalmist's assertion that man was given dominion over God's creation) such as exists also in Guatemala, but notions of Christian theocracy are no more practical in the Philippines than in Latin America. The Evangelicals, in any case, constitute no more than 10 per cent of the population.

A rather different pattern emerges in south **India**. Here there is no contiguous imperial presence to be blamed for cultural incursions. Nevertheless, the parallels with Latin America are striking. A considerable proportion of Christians is now associated with charismatic churches that emphasize the Bible and the gifts of the Spirit, including exorcism, healing, and prophecy. These churches are led by lay people rather than established hierarchies, and they seek out the supernatural in everyday life. As in Latin America, they offer opportunities for female participation. Parallel changes are taking place in the mainstream bodies, including the Roman Catholic Church. However, the mainstream bodies tend to look relativistic and compromising when faced with the militancy of Hindus and the power of non-Christian deities. What the new movements represent is the defense of the Christian stake in the social order, together with a specifically Indian reclamation of supernatural presences and powers.

Perhaps the most surprising contexts for these changes are in Western and Eastern Europe. In **Portugal**, for example, the rapid expansion of the Universal Church has made it second only to the Roman Catholic Church. The Universal Church appears to have an appeal for the educated young and has created a "People's Party." In

Hungary (which is perhaps more strictly Central than Eastern Europe) the Faith Church has become the fourth largest religious body in the country, after the Catholics, the Reformed, and the Lutherans. Its "prosperity gospel" has an extensive appeal among the Budapest middle class, and it has personnel links with the neo-liberal element in the current government.

A Look Into the Future

Thus far I have tried to characterize the Evangelical upsurge around the world, particularly in its social and political manifestations, and to give some examples of the varied forms it has taken. In this final section I will pick up some themes that bear on its future.

In his essay in this book, Peter Berger makes the point that the vitality of conservative religious groups in all three major monotheistic faiths is cognate with the relative decline of liberal groups that have attempted to conform to "modernity as defined by progressive intellectuals." At the same time, the major attempts in this century to institute what T. S. Eliot called "the idea of a Christian society" have all gone into decline. The Neo-Calvinist movement to constitute a specifically Christian culture was never very effective, whatever its intellectual underpinnings. Liberation theology was more effective in the proposals of its intellectual protagonists than in everyday reality, and it has declined since the arrival of Pope John Paul II and the passing of the Latin American political crises of the 1960s and 1970s. Christian Democracy always had a strong admixture of secularizing dynamism and is now, with the evanescence of dogmatic Communism, chronically lacking a plausible antagonist. This means that within societies with a Christian tradition, even in such strongly religious countries as the Irish Republic and Poland, the old inclusive frame allied to ecclesiastical monopoly is no longer viable. The Roman Catholic Church, even in Italy, accepts the fact that it cannot hope to dominate a society through a party such as "Democrazia Cristiana," and therefore sees itself as a potent commentator within a pluralistic framework, possessed at the same time of concrete institutional interests.

That role, the role of influential commentator within a pluralistic society, still exists, and it is probably the one that will eventually be taken up by the expanding Evangelical movements of the contemporary world. True, sometimes those movements are drawn by the cultural pull of the societies in which they operate to adopt corporatist models of intervention; sometimes they even entertain notions of replacing the Catholic Church in its old domination of public space. But that remains a dream. The likelihood is that Evangelicals will work within parties as commentators on the moral condition of society. In that respect Evangelical movements will exhibit a powerful contrast with those Islamic movements that seek the regulation of a whole society according to religious norms.

The Evangelicals' most potent contribution will be the creation of voluntary associations and the multiplication of social and political actors in the public arena. Other things being equal (which of course they rarely are), the cultural characteristics of Evangelicals—participation, pragmatism, competition, personal discipline—ought in the long run to foster democracy.

4

Judaism and Politics in the Modern World

Jonathan Sacks

The world is home to some 1.4 billion Christians, 800 million Muslims, and a mere 12 million Jews. Throughout the Diaspora, Jews are a tiny minority surrounded by large non-Jewish cultures. Israel is a tiny country surrounded by a vast constellation of Arab states. Jews are less than a quarter of a per cent of the population of the world. Our influence should be minimal.

But Jews and Judaism are of interest and influence in a way that numbers cannot account for. The American writer Milton Himmelfarb put it well: "Each Jew knows how thoroughly ordinary he is; yet taken together we seem caught up in things great and inexplicable. . . . The number of Jews in the world is smaller than a small statistical error in the Chinese census. Yet we remain bigger than our numbers. Big things seem to happen around us and to us."[1]

Let me begin at the beginning—the beginning, that is, of modern Jewish time, namely 1789, the year of the French Revolution and the birth of the modern secular nation-state. On August 26 the French

Jonathan Sacks is the Chief Rabbi of Britain and the Commonwealth. Previously he was the principal of Jews' College, London. He is the author of twelve books, including *The Persistence of Tradition*, *One People?*, and *The Politics of Hope*.

51

National Assembly issued its Declaration of the Rights of Man and of the Citizen, with its ringing opening assertion, "All men are born, and remain, free and equal in rights." Did that include Jews? Were Jews free? Were they equal? Were they citizens? Were they men?

The questions were real. At the very time of the declaration, anti-Jewish riots broke out in Alsace. This was an ominous indication that the secular nation-state might not end anti-Jewish sentiment but merely secularize it into a new mode, eventually to be given the name "anti-Semitism." Later that year, speaking in a debate over the eligibility of Jews for citizenship, the Count of Clermont-Tonnerre spelled out in a fateful sentence the terms on which Jews could be included in the new political dispensation. "The Jews," he said, "should be denied everything as a nation, but granted everything as individuals." He continued: "It is intolerable that the Jews should become a separate political formation or class within the country. Every one of them must individually become a citizen; if they do not want this, they must inform us, and we shall then be compelled to expel them."2

Thus was born what eventually became known as der Judenfrage, the "Jewish question," whose relatively innocent formulation gave rise, in 1941, to the Endlösung, the "final solution." The theory and terminology came from Germany. Some of the mythology, specifically the Protocols of the Elders of Zion, came from Russia. But it was in France, a century after the Revolution, that a Viennese journalist covering the Dreyfus trial, Theodore Herzl, came to the conclusion that there was no future for the Jews in Europe and that the secular nation-state, far from ending anti-Semitism, had in fact given it a new and potentially terrible rebirth. There was no future for the Jewish people, Herzl concluded, unless they constructed a nation-state of their own.

I go back to 1789 because contemporary discussions of Jewish life—issues like outmarriage, Jewish continuity, and Israel-Diaspora relations—often seem to me to lack depth because they lack a sense of historical background. There is a historical reason for this: the world's two greatest Jewries, Israel and the American Jewish community, are relatively recent phenomena, at least in their present size. Until 1840 almost 90 per cent of the Jewish world was to be found in Europe. Even more significantly, the Jews who made the journey to

America or Israel did so precisely to forget Europe, to break away from its prejudices and disabilities, and to make a new life in a new world. The strange contemporary blindness to Jewish history was born in a specific rebellion against Jewish history—a history that could be written in terms of wanderings and expulsions, inquisitions and pogroms, martyrdoms and exclusions, the powerlessness and homelessness of "the wandering Jew."

Against this I would argue that we cannot understand where we are unless we first understand how we came to be here. Israel cannot be understood as simply a secular democratic state on the European model; nor can the American Jewish community be understood within the standard parameters of American pluralism and denominationalism. These are part, but only part, of the Jewish story. The Israeli and American Jewish communities still carry within them the pains and tensions of the European Jewish experience, and even today they are shaped by what they were created to forget.

Two Crises for Modern Jewry

The modern Jewish experience has been deeply affected by two intellectual phenomena. The first is that Jews were, to use John Murray Cuddihy's phrase, "latecomers to modernity." There was no long prehistory, such as occurred in Christian Europe, of Renaissance, Reformation, the Wars of Religion, the birth of Enlightenment. Jews were thrust late into a complex set of challenges—the intellectual challenge of enlightenment, the political challenge of emancipation, and the social challenge of integration. What Jews believed, how they lived, and how they organized themselves came under sudden and concerted attack, sometimes in the name of progress, sometimes in the form of prejudice, and after centuries of exclusion from the mainstream of European culture they were radically unprepared to defend their beliefs and their way of life. This alone would have constituted a crisis of massive proportions for the continuity of Jewish faith.

It was, nonetheless, the lesser of two crises. The other, whose significance it is impossible to overstate, was the double bind of modernity itself as it affected European Jews, giving rise to the phenomenon eventually termed Jewish self-hatred. Sander Gilman described it in these terms:

On the one hand is the liberal fantasy that anyone is welcome to share in the power of the reference group if he abides by the rules that define that group. But these rules are the very definition of the Other. The Other comprises precisely those who are not permitted to share power within the society. Thus outsiders hear an answer from their fantasy: Become like us—abandon your difference—and you may be one with us. On the other hand is the hidden qualification of the internalized reference group, the conservative curse: The more you are like me, the more I know the true value of my power, which you wish to share, and the more I am aware that you are but a shoddy counterfeit, an outsider.[3]

This drama was played out again and again across Europe in the course of the nineteenth century, and the results were summed up by Max Nordau in his speech to the First Zionist Congress (1897). The "emancipated Jew in Western Europe," he said, "has abandoned his specifically Jewish character, yet the nations do not accept him as part of their national communities. He flees from his Jewish fellows because anti-Semitism has taught him, too, to be contemptuous of them, but his Gentile compatriots repulse him as he attempts to associate with them. He has lost his home in the ghetto, yet the land of his birth is denied to him as his home." Much has changed since those words were spoken a century ago, but we still live with their consequences.

The Enlightenment presented European Jews with a messianic promise and a demonic reality. The promise was a secular and rational order in which anti-Jewish prejudice would be overcome and Jewish civil disabilities abolished. The reality was that the more Jews became like everyone else, the more irrational and absolute became the prejudice against them: they were capitalists, they were Communists, they were too provincial and parochial, they were too rootless and cosmopolitan, they kept to themselves, they got everywhere, they were disloyal, they were suspiciously overloyal. The more assimilated they became, the more anti-Semitism grew.

A People or a Religion

The history of nineteenth-century Jewry is the tale of a dozen different attempts to find a way out of this Catch-22, from which there *was* no way out. The extreme response was a flight from Jewish identity through outmarriage, conversion to Christianity, or wherever possible the declaration that one was *Konfessionloss,* religionless. The Count of Clermont-Tonnerre had asked Jews to decide whether they were individuals or a nation—in other words, whether Judaism was a private religious confession or whether Jewry was essentially a collective entity, a people. Historically, of course, the answer was both; but the new European nation-state no longer permitted that reply.

Among those who shrank from the conclusion that Jews could survive only by ceasing to be Jews, there was a significant difference between Western and Eastern Europe. Faced with an either/or, in general the Jews of Western Europe decided in favor of Judaism as religion-without-peoplehood, those of Eastern Europe in favor of Jewry as peoplehood-without-religion. Hence there emerged in the nineteenth century a set of entirely new constructions of Jewish identity: in the West, Reform and Conservative Judaism; in the East, the movements for Jewish culture and even political autonomy in the Pale of Settlement. As these failed in their aims of normalizing Jewish existence, there emerged perhaps the greatest revolution in modern Jewish life: the Zionist movement, less an ideology than a collection of conflicting ideologies, some secular, some religious, some political, some cultural, some attempting to restore ancient traditions, others determined to destroy them completely and build a totally new kind of Jew.

The First Zionist Congress took place in 1897. A century later, we inhabit a Jewish world where in one sense everything has changed, and in another, nothing has changed. During the twentieth century, some of the most epic events in Jewish history have taken place— above all the Holocaust, the founding of the State of Israel, and the transfer of Jewish life from Europe to Israel and America. But the divisions in Jewish life today are almost exactly what they were a hundred years ago—between religious and secular; between Orthodoxy and Reform; and between those who see a Jewish future only in Israel and those who see a continuing role for the Diaspora. Between the first and the eighteenth centuries, with very few exceptions, a single Judaism prevailed: the Judaism of the Mishnah and Talmud, which today we call Orthodoxy. In the twentieth century, there has been no new Judaism. The apparent exception, the Reconstructionism of Mordecai Kaplan, was only a translation into the American context of the earlier ideas of Ahad Ha'am. So the immense diversity of answers to the questions "Who and what is a Jew?" all had their origin in a single century and continent: nineteenth-century Europe.

What, in 1897, were the various predictions about the Jewish future? Orthodox Jews believed that Reform would disappear: it was only a way-station on the road to total assimilation. Reform Jews believed that Orthodoxy would disappear: it was wholly incongruous with the modern world. Zionists believed the Diaspora would disappear: it was threatened equally by seduction and rape, assimilation and anti-Semitism. The non-Zionists believed that the hope of Jewish nationhood would disappear: the task of reviving an impulse buried for eighteen centuries was simply too great. We now know that every one of these predictions was wrong. Reform Judaism still exists. So does Orthodoxy. The state of Israel exists. The Diaspora survives. All those options in Jewish life that existed in 1897 exist today, and history has not yet delivered its verdict on any of them. The conflicts that, it was believed, would be resolved in the course of time have persisted and if anything intensified.

The Question of Jewish Unity

It is difficult to predict which conflict will be the most damaging—between Israel and the Diaspora, between secular and religious Israelis, or between Orthodox and Reform Jews outside Israel. Each of these groups denies the other's definition of reality, and the possibilities of dialogue are severely limited. Each rift has the potential of dividing Jewry irreparably into two. Five years ago when I published a book on Jewish unity entitled *One People?*, several friends in the United States wrote to me to say that it was a brave analysis but already too late. In America, in their view, Jews were no longer a single people. That has been the view of many Israelis about their own society for some time.

I am deeply concerned about these divisions, especially those in Israel, for an obvious reason. The Jewish people has often been threatened by hostile civilizations, from ancient Egypt, Assyria, Babylon,

Persia, Greece, and Rome to the Third Reich and the Soviet Union. But the most fateful injuries have been those the Jewish people has inflicted on itself: the division of the kingdom in the days of the First Temple, which brought about the eventual defeat of both halves and the loss of ten of the twelve tribes; and the internecine rivalry in the last days of the Second Temple, which brought about the destruction of Jerusalem and the longest exile in Jewish—indeed human—history.

There have been only three periods of Jewish sovereignty in four thousand years. Two ended in, and because of, internal dissension. The third age of sovereignty began in 1948, and already Israeli society is dangerously fragmented. Israelis themselves tend to downplay the danger. Even since the assassination of Prime Minister Yitzhak Rabin there has been too little effort at the highest levels to bring secular and religious groups together into some mode of mutual understanding. I believe this is a grave mistake, and I have said so to successive Israeli prime ministers and presidents. To survive, Israel must be not only a *medinah* but also a *chevrah,* not only a state but also a society. The democratic process alone does not guarantee the existence of a body politic. One needs in addition some minimal shared culture and identity. Israel at war is defined by its enemies. Israel in pursuit of peace is less easily defined, and more difficult to govern. That surely must be one concern for the future.

The Question of Jewish Continuity

Beyond the question of Jewish unity there is another contemporary anxiety, namely Jewish continuity. And here I come back to a point I made earlier, that current Jewish self-understanding is inhibited by a deliberate lack of historical awareness. In the 1990s, more has been written and spoken about Jewish continuity than any other Jewish topic, but with insufficient depth.

Jewish continuity is seen as a problem in the following terms. First, it is demographic: Jewish communities in the Diaspora are in decline, relative to Israel, relative to the larger societies of which they are a part, and even in absolute numbers. Second, it is a problem of outmarriage, most notably in the United States, where the 1990 National Jewish Population Survey showed that of the marriages of young Jews from 1985 to 1990, 52 per cent had been outmarriages where the non-Jewish spouse failed to convert. Third, it is a problem specifically of the Diaspora, not Israel, for two obvious reasons: Israel has grown, and outmarriage is not a significant problem in a country where Jews form a majority of the population. Fourth, the nature of the problem is defined in terms of the classic theory of the nation-state, whether in its American or its Israeli version. The American version is called the "melting pot." The United States is the place where from *pluribus* the *unum* forms, where immigrant communities inevitably assimilate. The Israeli version is called *shlilat hagolah,* negation of the Diaspora, which maintains that Jews can survive only within a predominantly Jewish society and culture.

I find these four characterizations inadequate. The problem of Jewish continuity is not first and foremost demographic. There were times, most notably after the Spanish expulsion, when the Jewish population fell to one sixth of what it is today, yet the same concerns were not expressed about the future survival of Jews and Judaism. Nor is it simply a problem of outmarriage. It is a problem also of non-marriage, late marriage, and low birthrates. And, as recent research by Charles Liebman and Steven M. Cohen has shown, outmarriage is not evenly distributed throughout the Jewish community. Reanalyzing the data of the 1990 National Jewish Population Survey, and categorizing Jews as actively, moderately, loosely, or not engaged, they discovered that the outmarriage figures were: among the actively engaged, 4 per cent; among the moderately engaged, 10 per cent; among the loosely engaged, 19 per cent; and among the disengaged, 49 per cent. Outmarriage is thus only a symptom of the larger problem of disaffiliation.

More controversially, I would argue that the problem of continuity is global and affects Israel no less than the Diaspora. Several surveys in the past few years have shown an alarming deracination among young Israelis—lack of knowledge of, and interest in, the Jewish heritage. This has translated itself into a significant body of Israeli thought known as post-Zionism, which would see Israel not as a Jewish state but as *medinat kol ezrachehah,* a "state of all its citizens." This would involve abandoning the Law of Return, rewriting the national anthem, the *Hatikva,* and severing links, not only with Jews worldwide, but also with Israel's biblical past and Judaic culture. At present Israel faces only a small problem of mixed marriage, but it is difficult to see how this could survive any genuine peace and interaction with its neighbors. There is collective as well as individual assimilation, and what appears in the Diaspora in the form of outmarriage appears in Israel in the form of secularization.

If therefore the problem is global, it is not to be understood in terms of the dynamic of the nation-state. Jews in the Diaspora do not inevitably disappear. Even a moderate degree of religious observance or communal affiliation guards against outmarriage. And even a state in which the majority of inhabitants are Jews does not of itself ensure the continuity of Judaism.

I therefore come back to my earlier analysis. The problem of Jewish continuity was born, not recently, but in the early days of the Jewish encounter with modernity. The most acute remark was made long ago by Mordecai Kaplan in the opening sentence of his book *Judaism as a Civilization:* "Before the beginning of the nineteenth century all Jews regarded Judaism as a privilege; since then most Jews have come to regard it as a burden." I would put it more pointedly still. Until the beginning of the nineteenth century, Jews defined themselves as the people loved by God. Since then most Jews, wittingly or unwittingly, have defined themselves as the people hated by Gentiles. No burden, especially the burden of being hated, is something decent people want to see handed on to their children. That may be why we have had so few Jewish children.

Defining Jewish Identity

Consider the most salient definitions of Jewish identity today. In Israel, as expressed by writers such as Amos Oz, it consists in living in a secular democratic state guided by the principles of the Enlightenment. In the United States, a famous survey conducted in Los Angeles in 1988 found that in answer to the question "which qualities do you consider most important to your Jewish identity?" 59 per cent replied, "a commitment to social equality." A mere 17 per cent chose "religious observance."[4] Nothing could be more striking than the fact that a people whose very *raison d'être* in the past was to be different, chosen, particular, should today define itself in purely universalist terms, forgetting—surely not accidentally—that it is precisely in our particularity that we enter and express the universal human condition. I am reminded of a remark made by the late Shlomo Carle-bach after a lifetime of visiting American campuses: "I ask students what they are. If someone gets up and says, 'I'm a Catholic,' I know that's a Catholic. If someone says, 'I'm a Protestant,' I know that's a Protestant. If someone gets up and says, 'I'm just a human being,' I know that's a Jew."

The seminal Jewish experience for the past two centuries has been what I call the "flight from particularity." It was born in the double bind of Jewish identity in Europe in the nineteenth century, and to-day both the Israeli and the American Jewish community are its heirs. Some Jews set themselves the self-conscious goal of ceasing to be Jews or ensuring that their children would not be Jews, whether through conversion or outmarriage or other forms of disaffiliation. Most Jews did not decide to cease being Jews. But they set them-selves two other goals, one more modest, the other more radical. The first was to be less conspicuous as Jews. Hence Sidney Morgan-besser's wonderful definition of Jewish identity as *incognito ergo sum*. In the Diaspora, that involved lowering the ritual content of Jewish life. In Israel it involved the pursuit of a new identity *kechol hagoyim*, "like all the nations." The second goal was to work for a world where religious differences no longer made a difference. Hence the essen-tially anti-religious liberalism that runs like a thread through Jewish intellectual life, from Spinoza to Amos Oz and Alan Dershowitz.

What is remarkable about both the Israeli and the American Jewish community is that in both countries, Jews are markedly more secular than their neighbors, be they Christian or Muslim. For four thousand years Jews were a people in search of God. Today Jews, more than any other group in the Western world, are a people trying to escape from God. Given the pain and tragedy of Jewish life for the past two centu-ries, indeed the past two millennia, that is not surprising. But it sug-gests that the crisis of Jewish continuity is due not to the failure but precisely to the success of Jewish strategies. As the Talmud records of a much earlier crisis in Jewish life, during the Hadrianic persecutions, "By rights we should issue a decree not to get married and have chil-dren, and let the seed of Abraham come to an end of its own accord." What Jewry faces today is a failure of the will that sustained our ances-tors across the generations: the willingness to be human by being dif-ferent and thus testifying to the dignity of difference.

Some Reasons for Hope

What is likely to be the outcome? I don't know. There is a difference between prediction and prophecy, just as there is a difference between optimism and hope. Certainly in the immediate future the Diaspora will decline in numbers. In Israel and America, Orthodoxy will grow. Other groupings will feel threatened by this growth, and there may be angry confrontations. Israel's dependence on financial and political support from the Diaspora will diminish, but that dependence is already minimal, and rightly so, because no sovereign state should have its domestic policies determined by those who do not live there. It may well be that politically, Israel and the Diaspora will drift apart. That will worry those who see the relationship as primarily political. It will give less concern to those who do not.

Speaking personally, though I am not an optimist, I am nonetheless full of hope. I see a new generation of Jews emerging, for the first time in many generations, with an undamaged, uncomplicated sense of Jewish identity. They recognize Judaism's spiritual power and moral grandeur. They are searching for personal meaning, moral guidance, and stability and structure in their lives. They have been touched by the outreach movements, and they are beginning to reconnect with Jewish observance and Talmud Torah, the study of Jewish texts. Almost every adult-education program we run in Anglo-Jewry is today oversubscribed, and there is a huge demand for new Jewish day schools.

This new generation, though personally committed to Orthodoxy, is far less interested in waging war with Reform—it is more secure, less easily threatened, more interested in opening the sources of Judaism to everyone than in building defensive walls. At long last it has moved beyond the vicarious sources of Jewish identity—anti-Semitism, the Holocaust, and support for Israel—toward a genuine personal encounter with the elements of Judaism that made it a source of inspiration for a hundred generations. Prominent among these are its love of family, community, education, and philanthropy, and its way of translating abstract ideals into simple daily practices: *kashrut,* the dietary rules; the observance of *shabbat,* the Sabbath; the sanctity of family life; and the choreography of *kedushah,* the distinct Jewish pattern of acts and observances that lead to a life of holiness.

Demographically, Diaspora communities will continue to decline for a while, but they will reach a plateau and then begin to grow again. We know from all recent research that the single greatest influence on whether we will have Jewish grandchildren is religious observance in the home: our British data suggest that this outweighs any other influence by a factor of at least five to one. Even a simple act like lighting candles on Friday evening makes a difference. There is a core of committed Jews in all major Diaspora Jewries, and they will not decline in numbers. The Diaspora is not about to disappear.

But the Jewish community, especially in the United States, may have to rethink its approach to politics. The American Jewish community is unusual in that it has based its influence, whether on Washington or on Israel, on demographic and financial power. Politically it has acted as a pressure group. The European Jewish model was quite different. It used the instrumentalities of *shtadlanut*, personal relationships and informal influence, neither of which depends on the numerical size of the community. American Jews may have to relearn this style.

The American Jewish community will continue to have an influence on Israel in the way it has in the past, which is not always the way it thinks it has. Its real contribution has not been money, or the sway it has exercised over U.S. foreign policy, but the people who have gone to live there. Two of the most significant developments in Judaism this century, the *Hesder yeshivot* and the *Baal Teshuvah yeshivot*, religious seminaries for those who serve in Israel's armed forces and for those who are returning to tradition, have largely been led by American rabbis who live and work in Israel.

What all of us will have to relearn is the fundamental truth with which I began. Jewish influence has never been based on numbers. In the last year of his life Moses told the Israelites, "God did not set his love on you and choose you because you were more numerous than other peoples, for you were the fewest of all peoples" (Deut. 7:7). Jews have had an influence out of all proportion to their numbers because of their loyalty to God, their commitment to a morally ordered society built on justice and compassion, and their courage in being true to their heritage while enhancing the lives of others.

The idea that nearly destroyed us as a faith in the nineteenth century was that Jews could solve the problem of anti-Semitism. The truth is that only anti-Semites can solve the problem of anti-Semitism. We can be vigilant against it, but we must never internalize it and let it affect our self-identity. It is time for us to stop defining ourselves as the people hated by Gentiles. Perhaps it is even time for us to re-establish our dialogue with God.

The Holocaust and the birth of Israel, the two most significant Jewish events of the twentieth century, both had their origins in a single concept—the nation-state. It was the nation-state that gave rise to the "Jewish question"—what to do with a minority that was different. And it was the nation-state that gave rise to the most powerful Jewish answer, namely, that Jews must have a state of their own. There is every indication that the twenty-first century, with its worldwide communications, multinational corporations, and international lobbies, will be one in which identities will no longer be defined by the nation-state. They will be both more local and more global—built around communities on the one hand, international communication on the other. Historically that is what the Jewish people has always been: a global people built around strong local communities. The Israel-Diaspora relationship will be transformed by this change. If the focus of the twentieth century was the Jewish state, in the twenty-first century it will be the Jewish people.

To sum up: just as Jews were latecomers to modernity, so we have been latecomers to post-modernity. Alone among the faith communities of the world, Jews welcomed secularization. It seemed to promise an end to religion, and therefore to religious persecution. In a sense it fulfilled the first part of that promise; but persecution persisted, only now without the restraints of religion. Jews have been living for some time in a condition of ambivalence about themselves and trauma about their relationship with the world. But time heals. And the Jewish people has never failed to recover from catastrophe. We are an ancient people, twice as old as Christianity, three times as old as Islam. And if history teaches us anything it is this, that Judaism survives not by numbers but by the quality and strength of Jewish faith. We always were an obstinate people, too obstinate to let go of God, and too obstinate to be defeated by history.

5

Europe: The Exception
That Proves the Rule?

Grace Davie

In considering the impact of religious conviction on world politics, it is hard to present the European case without appearing as something of a ghost at the feast. In a world characterized by religious resurgence rather than increasing secularization, Western Europe bucks the trend; or, to echo the point made in Peter Berger's essay, in Western Europe—if nowhere else—the "old" secularization thesis would seem to hold. To a considerable extent the data that follow will confirm that point. But it will later become clear that several explanations of these data are possible, and that the last of these may lead to a more nuanced interpretation. Might it not be the case that Europeans are not so much *less* religious than citizens in other parts of the world as *differently* religious? If so, the implications for public policy may well be considerable.

What do the countries of Western Europe have in common from a religious point of view? First among the several ways of looking at this question is a crucial historical perspective. James O'Connell,

Grace Davie is a senior lecturer in sociology at the University of Exeter. Her book *Religion in Modern Europe: A Memory Mutates* will be published by Oxford University Press. She is also the author of *Religion in Britain Since 1945: Believing Without Belonging.*

among others, identifies three formative factors or themes that come together in the creation and re-creation of what we call Europe: Judeo-Christian monotheism, Greek rationalism, and Roman organization.[1] These factors shift and evolve over time, but their combinations can be seen forming and re-forming a way of life that we have come to recognize as European. The significance of the religious strand within such combinations is evident.

But it is equally important to grasp from the outset the historical complexity of European identity. O'Connell approaches this by introducing seven interlocking and overlapping blocs that exist within the European whole: the western islands, western Europe, the Rhinelands, the Nordic/Baltic countries, the Mediterranean group, the former Ottoman territories, and the Slav peoples. While not all of these blocs will concern us here, the "building bloc" approach underlies a crucial aspect of modern as well as historical Europe. "If I have taken this building bloc approach," explains O'Connell, "it is to make clear, on the one hand, how closely knit Europe comes out of its history and how important it may be to make a future unity, and to suggest on the other hand, how complex Europe is and, in consequence, how varied might future unity mosaics prove to be."[2]

There is nothing deterministic about the future shape of Europe. Several approaches are possible, and so are several outcomes. Here we will stress one point in particular: the shared religious heritage of Western Europe as one of the crucial factors in the continent's development—and, possibly, in its future—and the influence of this heritage on a whole range of cultural values.

EXAMINING THE DATA

The 1981 and 1990 findings of the European Values System Study Group (EVSSG) are a principal source of data for this chapter.[3] In contrast with O'Connell's primarily historical approach, the European Values Study exemplifies, for better or worse, sophisticated social-science methodology.[4] Using careful sampling techniques, the EVSSG aims at an accurate mapping of social and moral values across Europe. It has generated very considerable data and will continue to do so, and we must pay close and critical attention to its findings.

Two themes run through the EVSSG study. The first concerns the substance of contemporary European values and asks, in particular, how homogeneous they are; the second takes a more dynamic approach, asking to what extent these values are changing. Both themes involve, inevitably, a religious element. The first, for example, leads very quickly to questions about the origin of shared value systems: "If values in Western Europe are to any extent shared, if people from different countries share similar social perceptions of their world, how had any such joint cultural experience been created?"[5] As the European Values Study indicates, the answer lies in deep-rooted cultural experiences deriving from pervasive social influences that have been part of our culture for generations, if not centuries. Quite clearly, a shared Judeo-Christian heritage is one such influence.

This much is unproblematic and confirms O'Connell's historical conclusions. But as soon as the idea of value *change* is introduced, the situation becomes more contentious. Unavoidable questions present themselves. To what extent is the primacy given to the role of religion in the creation of European values still appropriate? Has not this role been undermined by secularization? Is it possible to maintain at the turn of the millennium that religion remains a central element of the value system? Surely the influence of religion is becoming increasingly peripheral within European society—or is it?

These questions will concern us in the later part of this chapter. First it is important to look at the principal findings of the 1981 and 1990 EVSSG surveys for a variety of religious indicators.[6] There are, broadly speaking, five such indicators within the data: denominational allegiance, reported church attendance, attitudes towards the church, indicators of religious belief, and religious disposition. These variables have considerable potential: they can be correlated with one another and with a wide range of socio-demographic data. In this respect the survey shows commendable awareness of the complexity of religious phenomena and the need to bear in mind more than one dimension of an individual's (or a nation's) religious life.

These religious indicators cluster into two types of variable: those concerned with feelings, experience, and the more numinous religious beliefs, and those that measure religious orthodoxy, ritual participation, and institutional attachment. It is the latter, the more orthodox indicators of religious attachment, that reveal a significant degree of secularization throughout Western Europe. The former, the less institutional indicators, indicate a considerable persistence of some aspects of religious life. The essentials of this contrasting information are presented in the tables on pages 69-70, reproduced from the EVSSG data. These tables can be used in two ways: either to indicate the overall picture of the continent or to exemplify some of the national differences.

Continent-Wide Trends

The European Values Study remains cautious about using the term secularization, even in regard to Western Europe, for the data are complex, even contradictory, and clear-cut conclusions are difficult.[7] Bearing this in mind—together with the clustering of the variables mentioned previously—we might more accurately say that Western Europeans are *unchurched* populations, rather than simply secular. For a marked falling-off in religious attendance (especially in the Protestant North) has not resulted, yet, in an abdication of religious belief. While many Europeans have ceased to participate in religious institutions, they have not yet abandoned many of their deep-seated religious inclinations.[8]

But the situation of "believing without belonging" (if such we may call it) should not be taken for granted; it must be examined and questioned. In parts of Eastern and Central Europe prior to 1989, for instance, the two variables were reversed, for the non-believer quite consciously used attendance at Mass as a way of expressing disapproval of an unpopular regime. Poland is the most obvious example of this phenomenon.

Probing the West European data more deeply, we find further evidence of consistency in the shapes or profiles of religiosity across a wide variety of European countries: religious factors correlate—to varying degrees—with occupation, gender, and age. (Social class as such is more problematic.) Particularly striking is the correlation with age, which raises again the matter of the future shape of European religion (see note 8). Indeed, it prompts the most searching question of the study: are we, in Western Europe, experiencing a permanent generational shift in religious behavior? The 1986 EVSSG findings suggest that we are: "Markedly lower church attendance, institutional attach-

TABLE 1: Frequency of Church Attendance, 1990 (%)

	At least once a week	Once a month	Christmas, Easter, etc.	Once a year	Never
EUROPEAN AVERAGE	29	10	8	5	40
CATHOLIC COUNTRIES					
Belgium	23	8	13	4	52
France	10	7	17	7	59
Ireland	81	7	6	1	5
Italy	40	13	23	4	19
Portugal	33	8	8	4	47
Spain	33	10	15	4	38
MIXED COUNTRIES					
Great Britain	13	10	12	8	56
West Germany	19	15	16	9	41
Netherlands	21	10	16	5	47
Northern Ireland	49	18	6	7	18

	Once a month or more
LUTHERAN COUNTRIES	
Denmark	11
Finland	—
Iceland	9
Norway	10
Sweden	10

SOURCES: Table adapted from Sheena Ashford and Noel Timms, *What Europe Thinks: A Study of Western European Values* (Aldershot: Dartmouth, 1992), 46; additional figures for the Lutheran countries from EVSSG data (see note 3).

TABLE 2: Extent of Religious Belief, 1990 (%)

Belief in:	God	A soul after death	Life	Heaven	The Devil	Hell	Sin	Resurrec- tion of the dead
EUROPEAN AVERAGE	70	61	43	41	25	23	57	33
CATHOLIC COUNTRIES								
Belgium	63	52	37	30	17	15	41	27
France	57	50	38	30	19	16	40	27
Ireland	96	84	77	85	52	50	84	70
Italy	83	67	54	45	35	35	66	44
Portugal	80	58	31	49	24	21	63	31
Spain	81	60	42	50	28	27	57	33
MIXED COUNTRIES								
Great Britain	71	64	44	53	30	25	68	32
West Germany	63	62	38	31	15	13	55	31
Netherlands	61	63	39	34	17	14	43	27
Northern Ireland	95	86	70	86	72	68	89	71
LUTHERAN COUNTRIES								
Denmark	64	47	34	10	8	19	24	23
Finland	76	73	60	31	27	55	66	49
Iceland	85	88	81	19	12	57	70	51
Norway	65	54	45	24	19	44	44	32
Sweden	15	59	38	12	9	3	31	21

SOURCES: Table adapted from Sheena Ashford and Noel Timms, *What Europe Thinks: A Study of Western European Values* (Aldershot: Dartmouth, 1992), 40; additional figures for the Lutheran countries from EVSSG data (see note 3).

ment, and adherence to traditional beliefs is found in younger compared with older respondents, and data from other sources support the
notion that these are not life-cycle differences."[9] The shape of European religion in the twenty-first century might be very different indeed, a possibility supported by the data from the 1990 study.

So much for the similarities across Western Europe. What about
the differences? The most obvious is the difference between the notably more religious and Catholic countries of southern Europe and
the less religious countries of the Protestant north. This variation
holds across almost every indicator. Levels of practice, for example,
remain markedly higher in Italy, Spain, Belgium, and Ireland (closer
in its religious life to continental Europe than to Britain) than elsewhere. Not surprisingly, one effect of regular Mass attendance has
been a strength in the traditional orthodoxies through most of Catholic Europe.[10]

But there are exceptions. France, for example, displays a very different profile from that of the other Catholic countries, a contrast
that cannot be explained without reference to the history of the
country. Other exceptions—notably, the countries that do not conform to the "believing without belonging" framework at all—should
also be viewed from a historical perspective. Conspicuous here are
the two Irelands, where religion has become entangled with questions of Irish identity on both sides of the border. The high levels of
religious practice and belief in both the Republic and Northern Ireland are both cause and consequence of this entanglement. In the Republic especially, the statistics of religious practice remain unusually
high. (Within central Europe Poland shows a similar pattern.)

One further variation is important. In France, Belgium, the Neth-
erlands, and possibly Britain (more especially England), there is a
higher than average incidence of no religion, or at least no denominational affiliation. Indeed, Jean Stoetzel—in the French version of the
1981 EVSSG analysis—distinguishes four rather than three European types of religious affiliation: the Catholic countries (Spain, Italy,
and Eire); the predominantly Protestant countries (Denmark, Great
Britain, and Northern Ireland); the mixed variety (West Germany);
and what he calls a *région laïque,* that is, France, Belgium, the Nether-
lands, and, possibly, England, where those who recognize no religious label form a sizable section of the population.[11] In many ways

this analysis is more satisfying than the groupings suggested in the European Values material, where countries with very different religious profiles are lumped together.

These variations suggest one of the severest limitations of the EVSSG material: there is no way of telling from the data why a particular country should be similar to or different from its neighbors. Apparently similar statistical profiles can mask profound cultural differences. A second limitation lies in the fact that the EVSSG sample sizes for each country are too small to give any meaningful data about religious minorities. Yet it would be grossly misleading to present an image of Europe at the end of the twentieth century without reference to these increasingly important sections of the population.

Europe's Religious Minorities

The first of these minorities, the Jews, has been present in Europe for centuries. Its presence has been inextricably bound up with the tragedies of recent European history. Regrettably, moreover, anti-Semitism cannot be said to be a thing of the past; it continues to rear an ugly head from time to time right across Europe, an accurate indicator of wider insecurities. There are around one million Jews in Western Europe, the largest communities being the French (500,000-600,000) and the British (300,000). French Judaism has been transformed in the post-war period by the immigration of considerable numbers of Sephardim from North Africa.[12]

Former colonial connections also account for other non-Christian immigrations into Europe, most significantly the Islamic communities, though Britain also houses considerable numbers of Sikhs and Hindus. Islam is the largest other-faith population in Europe; conservative estimates suggest a figure of 6 million.[13] Muslims make up approximately 3 per cent of most West European populations.[14] The links between France and North Africa account for the very sizable French Muslim community (3-4 million), while Britain's equivalent comes from the Indian subcontinent (1.2 million). Germany has absorbed large numbers of migrant workers from the fringes of southeast Europe, and from Turkey and Yugoslavia in particular. (The fate of these migrants as more and more ethnic Germans look for work in the new Germany remains uncertain.)

Clearly, the Islamic presence in Europe is here to stay, and it follows that Europeans can no longer distance themselves from the debates of the Muslim world. This has crucial implications for public policy. Whether Europeans like it or not, whether they admit it or not, the issues are present on their own doorstep. Peaceful coexistence between Islam and Judeo-Christian Europe cannot be taken for granted. Nor can Muslims accept unequivocally the relatively secularized attitudes assumed by the majority of contemporary Europeans. This, surely, remains the problem at the heart of both the controversy surrounding the publication of Salman Rushdie's *The Satanic Verses* and the French equivalent of this controversy, the *Affaire du Foulard*.

One further source of diversity is the presence of new religious movements in all European societies. Their significance remains controversial. While these new movements attract considerable media attention (often negative), the numbers involved are tiny. Still, such movements fulfill an important function for the sociologist of religion as barometers of the changes taking place in society.[15] This perspective can be used to examine one of the most urgent public-policy challenges facing Europe today: the need to create and to sustain a truly tolerant and pluralist society, both in Europe as a whole and in its constituent nations. Such a society must go well beyond an individualized live-and-let-live philosophy. It must be able to accommodate what Oliver Leaman called "that unusual phenomenon" in contemporary Europe, the person (of whatever faith) who takes religion seriously.[16] The divergent postures displayed towards new religious movements by various European countries reveal underlying attitudes. If a country "fails" to accept new religious movements, it is unlikely, or at least very much less likely, to succeed in accepting other, considerably larger religious minorities.

INTERPRETING THE DATA

Now that we have surveyed the data, what do they suggest about the influence of religious conviction in European societies at the end of the century? I would like to offer three possible ways of interpreting the data, the last of which offers an innovative approach to European specificity. All three represent relatively recent sociological writing, though they draw on the more familiar texts that deal with secularization. Each takes note of the changing nature of European religion, but the three differ considerably in their explanations for this change and their predictions of the future.

The Secularization Thesis: Steve Bruce

Steve Bruce offers a classic statement—or restatement—of what has become known as the secularization thesis.[17] Building on the work of the founding fathers of sociology, together with that of Talcott Parsons, Peter Berger,[18] David Martin,[19] and Bryan Wilson,[20] Bruce sets out with admirable clarity what he feels to be the necessary connections between the onset of modernity and the demise of traditional forms of religious life. The key is to be found in the Reformation, which hastened the rise both of individualism and of rationality, currents that were to change the nature of religion and its place in the modern world. Bruce expresses these essential connections, the basis of his argument, as follows: "[I]ndividualism threatened the communal basis of religious belief and behavior, while rationality removed many of the purposes of religion and rendered many of its beliefs implausible."[21] The two, individualism and rationality, go together and epitomize the nature of modern cultural understanding.

The process should not be oversimplified; it is both complex and long term. Yet an underlying pattern can be discerned, one that took four centuries to complete. For at least three of these centuries, religious controversy dominated much of Europe's political, military, and cultural life; it took the form of competing convictions about the nature of God and his relationship to the individual believer (notably, Catholic and Protestant understandings of the only way to salvation). This is the period associated with the emergence of the nation-state as the effective form of political organization in Europe. Gradually a *modus vivendi* emerged, as greater toleration of difference become the norm both within and between the states of Europe.

But toleration is two-edged; it implies, following Bruce, a lack of conviction, a live-and-let-live capacity that becomes not only dominant but pervasive. A further epistemological shift seems inevitable. In the late modern period, the concept of God, *him*self or *her*self, becomes increasingly subjective; individuals simply pick and choose from the diverse views on offer. Religion, like so many other things, has entered the world of options, life-styles, and preferences. The great majority of people not only reject serious convictions for themselves but find them difficult to comprehend in others. Religious institutions evolve accordingly: church and sect give way, in Bruce's terminology, to denomination and cult—forms of religious organization that reflect the increasing individualism of religious life. Notably absent is the overarching "sacred canopy," to use Peter Berger's term, the all-encompassing religious frame expressed organizationally as the universal church. This concept no longer resonates in the modern world.

But what do we mean by the "modern world"? Bruce is concerned with modern societies insofar as these display basically egalitarian cultures and democratic politics.[22] In other words, he is concerned with modern Western democracies, including Europe (for the most part Western Europe), the United States, and the English-speaking dominions (Canada, Australia, and New Zealand). He makes passing reference to Latin America. Even this relatively limited selection of societies reveals, however, widely different religious profiles. At one extreme can be found the Protestant cultures of Northern Europe with their tolerant and well-funded state churches, co-existing with low levels of religious practice and only moderate levels of religious belief (Sweden especially epitomizes these characteristics). At the other extreme lies the United States, also Protestant in culture but with an astonishing range of vibrant churches alongside extraordinarily (from a European point of view) high levels of religious belief. In between can be found (a) the Catholic cultures of Southern Europe, rather more intact than their Protestant neighbors but with historically strong oppositional or anti-clerical tendencies, and (b) the English-speaking dominions, whose position is halfway between those of Europe and the New World. It follows that even within modern Western democracies, individualism and rationality appear to have different outcomes in different places, and they are not necessarily linked with each other.

A second question immediately presents itself. Can one theoretical approach account for a range of outcomes as great as this, never mind the innovative hybrids currently emerging in Latin America, which is beginning to look more like the United States than Latin Europe? Two of Bruce's mentors—Peter Berger[23] and David Martin[24]—have posed just this question concerning the secularization thesis and have revised their opinions accordingly. Both focus on the concept of "exceptionalism."

The secularization thesis developed within a European framework, and for certain stages in Europe's religious development there is a convincing fit between the argument and the data. As Europe's economic and political life developed, religion diminished in public significance; religious aspirations were increasingly relegated to the private sphere. Bit by bit, however, the thesis rather than the data began to dominate the agenda. The "fit" became axiomatic, theoretically necessary rather than empirically founded—so much so that Europe's religious life was considered a prototype of global religiosity: what Europe did today, everyone else would do tomorrow. Secularization was a necessary part of modernization, and as the world modernized, it would automatically secularize.

But if this was so, how could the very different situation in the United States be explained? The answer lay in trying to understand American exceptionalism; i.e., in realizing that America was different and looking for particular aspects of American society that could account for the successful cohabitation of vibrant religiosity and developed modernity. So far, so good; the secularization thesis remains intact even if deviations can be found.[25]

But not everyone has continued down this path. Berger and Martin, for example, have suggested that the argument be reversed. Exceptionalism undoubtedly exists, but it is Europe rather than the United States that is exceptional. Not only, following Berger, is the non-Western world as "furiously religious as ever,"[26] but the United States itself continues by all conventional criteria to be an intensely religious country. So what happens to the argument about relativism breeding secularity? In the United States it simply has not happened. What has emerged, rather, is a healthy and competitive market of religious institutions, some of which appear to be thriving more than others. Paradoxically, it is the more conservative religious groups that attract the greater numbers of religious adherents in this liberal era. Those that resist compromise most successfully seem to flourish in a culture of increasing uncertainty.

Where does this leave the question of European—as opposed to American—forms of religion? They must be seen, surely, as one strand among the many that make up what it means to be European. European religion is not a model for export; it is something distinct, peculiar to the European corner of the world. What this religion is like in the latter part of the twentieth century and what it may be like in subsequent decades are questions that require further study.[27]

Religion in the Modern World: José Casanova

A second attempt to understand the nature of secularization and how the concept applies to European society can be found in the work of José Casanova.[28] Casanova agrees that the paradigm of secularization has been the main theoretical frame through which the social sciences have viewed the relationship of religion and modernity. Part of the confusion about the results, he thinks, lies within the concept itself, which must be clarified before the debate can be taken any further. Casanova attempts to provide this clarification as his starting point:

> A central thesis and main theoretical premise of this work has been that what usually passes for a single theory of secularization is actually made up of three very different, uneven and unintegrated propositions: secularization as differentiation of the secular spheres from religious institutions and norms, secularization as decline of religious beliefs and practices, and secularization as marginalization of religion to a privatized sphere. If the premise is correct, it should follow from the analytical distinction that the fruitless secularization debate can end only when sociologists of religion begin to examine and test the validity of each of the three propositions independently of each other.[29]

Secularization as a concept is to be not abandoned but refined, making possible a more accurate analysis of religion in different parts of the world.[30]

Casanova offers five case studies, two from Europe, two from the United States, and one from Latin America. Two points that emerge from these case studies are essential for an understanding of modern Europe. The first is that *secularization* as *differentiation* is the essential core of the secularization thesis. "The differentiation and emancipa-tion of the secular spheres from religious institutions and norms re-mains a general modern structural trend."[31] But modernity does not necessarily imply a reduction in the level of religious belief or prac-tice, nor does it imply that religion is necessarily relegated to the pri-vate sphere. Indeed, the intention of Casanova's book is not only to discover but also to affirm a legitimate *public* role for religion in the modern world, including modern Europe. The second point follows from this: those churches that have resisted the structural differentia-tion of church and state—notably the state churches of Europe—are the ones that have found it hardest to come to terms with the pres-sures of modern life-styles. Hence the decline of religious vitality in much of modern Europe. Rather than being an inevitable outcome of modernity, this decline results from the particular arrangements of church and state that predominate in European history. It is, follow-ing the central argument of this essay, a European phenomenon with a European explanation, not an instance of an axiomatic relation be-tween modernity and secularization in the world as a whole.

The two European case studies selected by Casanova provide con-trasting illustrations of this approach. The first, Spain, exemplifies the argument. Here the protracted—and tragic—resistance of the Catholic Church to modern forms of economic and political life has had profoundly negative consequences for religious life; only now can the Spanish church begin to shake off the associations of its past and come to terms with a modern democratic regime. The Spanish case is particularly instructive sociologically in that it is an artificially delayed and therefore speeded-up version of modernity, in which the competing tensions are unusually clear. What has taken a century in most parts of Europe has happened within a generation in Spain. The statistics tell the same story: the drop in religious practice between the 1981 and 1990 European Values surveys was larger in Spain than anywhere else, and this is echoed by the drop in vocations to the priesthood.[32] A very significant generation gap is emerging.

In Poland there has been a different juxtaposition altogether. Here a powerful and increasingly monolithic church was the focus of re-sistance to, rather than the ally of, a state that itself lacked legitimacy. Resistance to secularization became associated in Poland with resis-tance to an illegitimate power; the combination strengthened rather than diminished the position of the Church and resulted in unusually high figures of religious practice throughout the Communist period. But what of the future? Since 1989 the Polish church, like its Spanish counterpart, has faced a very different situation; it must now find its place in a modern democracy where a monolithic, semi-political presence (even one that could take pride in its resistance to Communism) is no longer sustainable. Paradoxically, the most powerful church in central Europe seems to be the one least able to trust itself to the democratic process.

Casanova makes almost no reference to the state churches of Northern Europe. Do these, too, exemplify resistance to the modern order and find themselves ill suited to the competitions of late capitalist society? Among those making this argument are some of the persons most active in such churches. This is certainly the case in the Church of England. Casting covetous eyes across the Atlantic, a vociferous minority of active Anglicans argues that deregulation of religion in the United States is a principal reason for religious vitality in the New World, so why not try the same formula in Northern Europe? From a sociological point of view, rational-choice theorists would support such a notion.[33] I am not so sure, however, for the hypothesis requires that all other things be equal, and here all other things clearly are *not* equal.

A more practical way forward lies in identifying—and from the point of view of the churches themselves, exploiting—the particularities of existing arrangements in Northern Europe where Protestant state churches coexist alongside moderately secular but far from oppositional cultures. This situation is rather different from the clerical–anti-clerical tensions of Latin Europe (so well described by Casanova), a contrast that can be explained ecclesiologically. In most of Northern Europe, Protestantism itself declericalized the Church; there was no need for an outside anti-clerical alternative. But how such churches should move forward within a modern democracy is, again, an open question.

Religion as Collective Memory: Danièle Hervieu-Léger

My third theoretical approach borrows from a leading French sociologist of religion, Danièle Hervieu-Léger, whose point of departure lies in trying to identify and refine the conceptual tools necessary to understand religion in the modern world.[34] An answer gradually emerges in the definition of religion as a specific mode of believing. The crucial points to grasp in this analysis are (a) the *chain* that makes the individual believer a member of a community—a community that gathers past, present, and future members—and (b) the *tradition* (or collective memory) that becomes the basis of that community's existence. Hervieu-Léger goes further than this: she argues that modern societies (and especially modern European societies) are less religious, not because they are increasingly rational, but because they are less and less capable of maintaining the memory that lies at the heart of their religious existence. They are—to use her own term— amnesiac societies. This is a rather different argument from one that assumes, uncritically, that European societies have found satisfactory alternatives to the traditional forms of religion so crucial in their historical formation. Manifestly, they have not.

Indeed, in an earlier book, Hervieu-Léger argues that modern societies are by their very nature corrosive of the traditional forms of religious life; she supports this argument with the kind of data presented earlier in this chapter, notably the fall in the hard indicators of religious activity.[35] In this sense the argument is reminiscent of Bruce's presentation of the secularization thesis. But it is only half the story. Modern societies may well corrode their traditional religious base, but at the same time they open up spaces or sectors that only religion can fill. These Hervieu-Léger refers to as "utopian" spaces. Modern individuals are encouraged to seek answers, to find solutions, and to make progress. Such aspirations become an increasingly normal part of human experience. But their realization must remain problematic, for the horizon will always recede. The image of utopia must always exceed reality, and the more successful the projects of modernity, the greater the mismatch becomes. Hence the paradox of modernity, which in its historical forms removes the need for and sense of religion (the "amnesia"), but in its utopian forms must stay in touch with the religious (the need for a religious future). Through what mechanisms, then, can modern European societies overcome their amnesia and stay in touch with the forms of religion that are necessary to sustain their identity? That seems to me the challenge set by Hervieu-Léger's analysis.

The more recent book by Hervieu-Legér, *La religion pour mémoire,* is an exacting one to read. It struggles with conceptual issues within the sociology of religion that have, from the outset, proved impossibly difficult to resolve—notably the definition of religion—and further difficulties will arise as her new formulations are applied. As we have seen, the proposed ideal type takes as its organizing axis some sort of reference to the legitimating authority of a tradition; this point of view postulates the existence of a believing community, either real or imaginary, that links the individual believer to something beyond his or her self. Such links become a chain of belief. But precisely which chains are to be included in the definition of religion and which are not will depend, once again, on the judgments of the observer. There are bound to be differences of opinion as disputed and marginal cases catch the attention of sociologists.

But the disputed and the marginal should not detract from the wider point. Hervieu-Léger's analysis offers a major step forward in the sociology of religion in that it provokes an immediate flood of pertinent questions, one of which has to do with regional, national, or international memories. A brief illustration—building on data presented in the first section of this chapter—will indicate the potential in this approach for a better understanding of European religion today.

Clearly, there have been times when a common memory molded the European continent into a unity in which secular and temporal power were barely distinguishable. Later centuries saw this common memory disintegrate into national and regional variations; competing religious memories became a crucial variable in emphasizing difference rather than commonality. In the 1990s, however, as steps are taken toward a unified Europe, the situation alters once again. All sorts of possibilities present themselves. Can the religious factor for example be used to emphasize what Europe has in common? Or will it be used, conversely, to provide support for discrete and independent nations, each with its own religious sphere, and possibly a national church? Either scenario is possible. But the argument can also be turned the other way round. The churches (national or otherwise), religious individuals, or a wide variety of religious organizations may attempt to initiate—rather than reflect—shifts in public opinion. In other words, the religious factor may operate as an independent variable, either in bringing about or in resisting a greater European consciousness.

Examining these possibilities within the framework elaborated by Hervieu-Léger seems to me a fruitful approach to some of the questions currently facing Europe. One might look, for example, at the essentially Catholic origins of European unity and the role of prominent Christian Democrats (such as Jean Monnet, Robert Schuman, and Alcide de Gasperi) in the creation of a European union. Given this scenario, it is hardly surprising that some nations in the Protestant North have been somewhat skeptical about what is going on. And what is relatively benign in most of them occasionally becomes very much less so—notably in Northern Ireland, where the matter is exacerbated by the relative success of Catholic Ireland, never mind Catholic Europe, within the emergent frameworks of European unity. From a rather different perspective, Orthodox Greece too has affirmed a distinct, non-Catholic national identity. And in the Balkans proper, the interrelationships of religious identity and a multiplicity of other factors become ever more difficult to disentangle; conflicting "memories" compete in their territorial claims, sometimes with devastating consequences.

Conclusion: Vicarious Religion

The Balkans remain, thankfully, an exceptional case, compared with the relative indifference of most West Europeans to serious considerations of religion. But amidst this indifference, the churches still function as a kind of "vicarious memory": a significant proportion of Europeans delegate to their churches, often state churches, what they no longer consider doing themselves. On the eve of the millennium, then, many Europeans remain grateful to rather than resentful of their churches, recognizing that the churches perform a number of tasks on behalf of the population as a whole. Churches are asked, for instance, to articulate the sacred at times in the life-cycle of individuals and families, and at times of national crisis or celebration.[36] A refusal to carry out these tasks would violate both individual and collective expectations.

Central to these equations are the relationships between active and passive groups. So far, enough of the religiously inactive in Europe have retained a nominal attachment to their churches that the churches' representative role is still possible. Indeed, in many respects that role is encouraged—whether in terms of worship, the life-cycle, ethical issues, or political debate. Whether this will remain true for much longer is an extremely pertinent question. One of the obvious risks of operating vicariously is the lack of direct contact between the churches and the population. While this may not result in an immediate loss of religious sensitivity (the data suggest otherwise), it does lead to a dramatic generation-by-generation drop in religious knowledge. An ignorance of even the basic understandings of Christian teaching is the norm in modern Europe, especially among young people; it is not a reassuring attribute.

6

The Quest for Meaning: Religion in the People's Republic of China

Tu Weiming

A n eminent scholar of Chinese thought, Professor Kong Fan, observed that in the 1950s the Chinese Academy of Social Sciences established an institute for the study of world religions against
the strong opposition of the Russian scholarly advisors. According to
the official Marxist ideology that was espoused in the Soviet Union,
religion is at most an epiphenomenon, if not "the opiate of the people." It is therefore neither necessary nor desirable to study religion
as a serious academic subject, because precise "scientific" methodology cannot be adequately applied. The Chinese counter-argument,
Kong Fan reported, was that religion *should* be taken seriously as a research topic, for not only do the Three Teachings—Confucianism,
Taoism, and Buddhism—define the salient features of Chinese spiritual civilization, but an appreciation of the religious factor is essential
for understanding each of the more than fifty officially recognized
minorities in China. Yet despite the scholarly contribution of the
Institute of World Religions, the Chinese political and intellectual

Tu Weiming is a professor of Chinese history and philosophy at Harvard
University and the director of the Harvard-Yenching Institute. Among his
publications are *Way, Learning, and Politics: Essays on the Confucian Intellectual,*
and *Centrality and Commonality: An Essay on Confucian Religiousness.*

elite's awareness of religion as an integral part of modern life has been at best superficial.

The emergence into prominence of Enlightenment values since the May Fourth Movement (1917-1921) has been instrumental in relegating religion in contemporary China to the backwaters of false beliefs and outright superstition. During the early decades of the twentieth century, the most influential Westernizers glorified democracy and science as the defining characteristics of modernity; they were convinced that populism and positivism were the wave of the future.

This may have been why, despite the slogan "wholesale Westernization," there was little enthusiasm for Christianity among the leading Westernizers. Many were openly hostile to missionary movements and condemned Chinese and foreign Christians' involvement in the modernization of China as part of an insidious conspiracy or blatant cultural imperialism.

The issue of the relevance of Christianity to China's modernization is, of course, immensely complex. Suffice it now to note that the main thrust of the Chinese intellectual value-orientation was so much shaped by the burning desire to (a) keep the imperialists at bay and (b) transform China into a modern nation that religion was variously misconstrued as a dispensable luxury, an outmoded way of life, a personal quest inimical to group solidarity, a negative dimension of the habits of the heart, a burden, or an archaic irrelevance. Hu Shi, the leading liberal and positivist thinker in modern China, proudly reported an eyewitness account that a missionary was unable to persuade an illiterate Chinese waiter to accept the Christian truth because he was unable to demonstrate God's existence to the satisfaction of the waiter, who demanded concrete proof. In a more serious vein, Hu Shi lamented the historical phenomenon that, prior to the impact of the West, China had been "Indianized" for centuries to become a Buddhist country. Hu Shi's delight in China's alleged rejection of Christianity and his lament over China's obvious acceptance of Buddhism are symptomatic of the intellectual disposition to view religion as, paradoxically, both inconsequential and incompatible with modernization.

The Turn to Populism and Positivism

The triumph of Marxism-Leninism in China, as a result of a complex interaction between iconoclasm and nationalism, signaled a new constellation in the Chinese intellectual skies: the belief that advanced Western thought—rather than indigenous spiritual resources—will bring about China's national reconstruction, and that China, despite its backwardness, will prevail over all the obstacles to become a modern civilization. This combination of profound self-doubt (none of our celebrated ancestors can help us now, so our survival is based on our courage to reject the past and embrace the brave new world) and equally profound self-confidence (we shall overcome!), contradictory as it was on the surface, helped to generate a dynamic process from which a powerful new consensus began to emerge. According to this, if the Chinese follow the Enlightenment project, defined in terms of democracy and science, they must, as a strategy though not necessarily a conviction, thoroughly identify themselves with populism and positivism. If the Chinese populace as a whole follows the most advanced "scientific" thinking about development, then tremendous energy will be released and will propel China from its miserable state as the "sick man of East Asia" to a position of wealth and power. As pragmatism, utilitarianism, materialism, and scientism soared in the ethos of the political leadership and intellectual elite, the voice of religion was overwhelmed by the hysteric cry to save the nation.

Ironically, the Chinese Communist movement led by Mao Zedong, a highly distorted version of the Enlightenment project, was inspired by revolutionary romanticism as well as by instrumental rationality, and a kind of religious fervor featured prominently in the process. The intellectual effervescence was fueled by Bakunin's anarchist sentiments rather than his utopian idea of mutual aid, by Marx's resentment against class exploitation rather than his analysis of the capitalist system, by Bacon's aggressive anthropocentrism rather than his inductive method, and by Rousseau's general will rather than his social contract. The revolutionaries believed that the harshness of the human condition demanded a tough-mindedness characteristic of guerrilla warfare and military confrontation. Matters of the heart were considered counterproductive in the fierce struggle for survival; sentimentalism was condemned as counterrevolutionary. As a result, the Confucian values of moderation, harmony, civility, and humaneness were rejected as incompatible with the spirit of the time.

A Crisis of Meaning

But lurking behind the apparent consensus was a crisis of meaning. Even those who were absolutely convinced that for the sake of national survival China had no choice but to follow the path of populism and positivism failed, often by deliberate choice, to become either populist or positivistic in their own life-styles. The leading liberal Hu Shi championed the cause of democracy and science, but he remained an elitist by arguing for the importance of "the politics of the worthies" *(xianren zhengzhi)* and scholarship in the humanities. He condemned Buddhism for its corrosive influence on the Chinese martial spirit, but he devoted much of his scholarly energy to Chan (Zen) studies. Although he never conceded his negative attitude toward all organized religions, Hu Shi addressed issues of immortality and concluded that while individuals could never achieve immortality, society could become everlasting.

The generation prior to the founding of the People's Republic of China (1949) eagerly debated the path to national salvation. The fear that China could disintegrate into a mere geographic expression was so intense that saving the country from foreign aggression and domestic implosion was the overriding concern. The major issues included the industrialization of an agriculture-based economy, the choice between socialism and capitalism, and the need to adopt Western science and technology without losing sight of the core values in Chinese culture.

Already the picture was much more complex than the simple-minded fusion of iconoclasm and nationalism. To be sure, the ascendancy of Marxism-Leninism indicates that the persuasive power of populism and positivism had extended way beyond intellectual circles to become a new ideology of revolutionary praxis. Mao's obvious success in using guerrilla tactics to enlarge the Communist base areas and in employing "class struggle" to mobilize the peasants should not blind us to the fact that it was the persistent support of a coterie of devoted intellectuals that enabled him to articulate his revolutionary vision on a national and, eventually, international stage. The question of meaning is again relevant here.

The party-line interpretation of Mao Zedong's thought as the guiding principle for China's modernization under the leadership of the Chinese Communist Party is simply that it has correctly and creatively integrated the universally valid revolutionary ideology imported from the Soviet Union into the specific local Chinese conditions. But the collapse of the Soviet system and the radical transformation of the Chinese economy seem to have rendered Maoism obsolete. Indeed, the bitter memory of the Cultural Revolution, often characterized as the "ten-year calamity" (1966-1976), must have thoroughly discredited Mao's alternative "modernist" model.

New Synthesis: The "Socialist Market Economy"

Nevertheless, the fear that a market economy with the inevitable consequence of democratization would restructure the entire society and thus shake the foundations of the party's leadership prompted Deng Xiaoping and his comrades to formulate a new ideological line: "socialist market economy," said to be a form of socialism with Chinese characteristics. It is easy for us to detect irreconcilable elements in such a synthesis and to dismiss it as a desperate attempt to give meaning to a disintegrating system. We need to remind ourselves, however, that the Beijing leadership under Jiang Zemin that emerged out of the Tiananmen tragedy (1989) has been muddling through reasonably well in managing China's economy, the return of Hong Kong (1997), and even the political move toward a more open and pluralistic society.

In a 1986 reflection on the religious situation in China I observed:

The upsurge of activity in organized religions is a reflection of China's open-door policy. As this policy continues, pluralism both as an ideological stance and as an experienced reality seems inevitable. The perceived danger of the vulgarization of culture, the disintegration of society (especially the family) and the destabilizing influence of the political structure, as the result of intensified contact with the outside world, will have an effect on the ability of the reformers to sustain high-level support in the ruling minority as well as among the people. The voice of the intelligentsia (the scholars, writers, journalists and those who are characterized as workers in the theoretical fields who are charged with the responsibility of fixing the superstructure) will be critical in setting up the agenda for and adjudicating unavoidable conflicts in determining the priority of values in China's changing, indeed restless ideological landscape.

Whether or not a new common creed will actually emerge, as the result of a confluence of many potentially contradictory streams of thought, the quest for a common creed despite pluralist tendencies will continue. This seems to be profoundly meaningful for students of religion. After all, the necessity for working toward a common creed in this pluralistic world of ours is urgent. The Chinese attempt is at least heuristically suggestive.[1]

With the hindsight of the Tiananmen tragedy, a sense of gravity overshadows any naïve optimism that the "muddling through" will work reasonably well for years to come. It is hard to imagine any encouraging scenario, given the major flood in the summer of 1998 (attributable to the man-made environmental disasters of deforestation and the conversion of major lakes along the Yangtze to farmland), the internal migration of over 100 million workers from rural to urban areas, and the deepening of the Asian economic crisis.

Since the Opium War in the mid-nineteenth century, China has suffered innumerable calamities. The Taiping Rebellion that cost an estimated 20 million lives (1851-64), the Japanese aggression with casualties of more than 30 million civilians (1937-45), and the devastating policy after the Great Leap Forward that resulted in the death by starvation of as many as 40 million (1962-65)—these are, by any measure, major tragedies in the violent history of the modern world. But while people in China suffered, its neighboring states were not directly affected, and the rest of the world was largely oblivious to what had happened.

Since 1979, China has increasingly become an integral part of the global community. Already more than 30 per cent of the Chinese economy is tied to international trade. As investors, business people, tourists, journalists, diplomats, and scholars from Taiwan, Hong Kong, overseas Chinese communities, Japan, the United States, and the European Community begin to visit virtually all provinces in China, and as Chinese students, researchers, government officials, sightseers, and immigrants begin to make their presence known throughout the world, what is happening in China will have a major impact on East Asia, the Asia-Pacific realm, and the international community as a whole. What cultural message, if any, is embedded in the rise of China as a military, political and economic power? This question is no longer insignificant for the global community. A general survey of the religious landscape in China may give us a glimpse of a possible answer to this immensely complex question.

The Christian Influence in China

The general impression that the crisis of meaning has made China a fertile land for religion is basically sound, but the exaggerated claim that China is well on its way to becoming the Elysian fields for Christian evangelism needs elucidation. Surely, one of the most notable developments in religion is the spread of Christianity among peasant communities as well as in elite intellectual circles. Both Protestantism and Catholicism have made substantial inroads in Chinese society across boundaries of gender, race, income, region, education, profession, and age. But if we refine the categories of investigation, the picture is far from clear. Among rural converts, the main thrust of Christian evangelism has come from indigenous missionaries, or, more precisely, ethnic Chinese dialect-speaking preachers, some of whom came from Taiwan, Hong Kong, Macao, Singapore, and other overseas Chinese communities. Building upon the foundation of native Chinese churches, this movement, basically Pentecostal in nature, has been so seasoned by the local conditions that it is very unlike the practice of Christianity elsewhere. Both its way of operating and its spiritual ethos are nativistic to the core, and there is often a streak of anti-foreignism in its message.

The university students, professionals, social activists (especially those involved in the pro-democracy movement), and business executives who have converted to Christianity symbolize an urban phenomenon in sharp contrast to the rural scene. Not unlike the situation in Singapore, these newly emerged Chinese Christians style themselves as cosmopolitan, Westernized reformers. Some of them perceive a natural fit between Christianity and science, technology, and democracy. This reminds us of the "golden age" of the Christian movement in China during the Republican period (1927-49), when, under the influence of Madame Chiang Kai-shek (Jiang Jieshi) and the Song family, the Nationalist leadership was hospitable to the Christian Gospel, notably as presented by the Methodists. Against this political backdrop, the Christian contribution to China's modern transformation in education, medicine, banking, industry, science, technology, charitable organization, and civil society in general has been extensive. Let us look at just one aspect, higher education.

It is widely known that Christian universities, such as Yenching, Chinling, St. Johns, Lingnan, Fujen, and Soochow, were instrumental in developing an American style of teaching and research in Republican China. While national universities, notably Peking, Nankai, Fudan, and Central, may have produced more political leaders, graduates from the Christian universities provided important human resources for virtually all professions. Furthermore, by emphasizing a liberal arts education, Christian universities trained several generations of modern scholars in the humanities and social sciences. Although all Christian universities were outlawed with the founding of the People's Republic, their alumni, numbering in the thousands, continued to play a vital role in many fields, including economics, diplomacy, education, and journalism. Despite Zhou Enlai's critique of American cultural imperialism, the legacy of the Christian influence on Chinese higher education is indelible. Major universities in China such as Peking, Nanjing, Beijing Normal, and Zhongshan are clearly indebted to—respectively—the former Yenching, Chinling, Fujen, and Lingnan universities for their facilities and faculties.

To be sure, the Christian contribution to China's higher education did not automatically lead to the spread of Christianity in China, but it enabled Chinese Christians to find a niche in the nation's quest for modernization. Furthermore, it created a symbolic space for Christian intellectuals to express their ideas as legitimate concerns of a new China. After all, ever since the mid-nineteenth century, Christians have been champions of woman's liberation, medical care for the poor, human rights, and philanthropy.

However, in the current political climate in mainland China, behind all the positive images of Christianity, the memory of cultural imperialism—or, in its more invidious contemporary disguise, the strategy of deconstructing the official ideology through "peaceful transformation"—still looms large in the minds of those who are responsible for charting China's socialist course. A case in point is the conflict between the government-sanctioned patriotic priests and the underground Catholic organizations recognized by the Vatican as true representatives of the Christian faith. Beijing's religious leadership insists that financial, doctrinal, and organizational independence is a minimum condition for establishing an institutional base for spreading religious teaching. Theoretically, freedom of assembly is governed by a hierarchy of control that does not allow any unattached groups to operate as voluntary associations. Even nongovernmental organizations are officially registered bodies under the supervision of a particular unit. This is true for all legitimate Christian groups. In practice, since the regulatory mechanism is quite flexible, all sorts of group activities are permissible. Only when they are perceived as threatening to public security will the authority make its presence known. Yet the arbitrariness in interpreting the range of permissibility makes the freedom of religion as well as the freedom of assembly highly problematical.

There is no reliable account of the actual number of Christians in China today; the figures vary widely. The estimate of 70 million made by some underground Christian groups is at least three times as high as the official estimate. More significant is the rate of growth. Even though the claim that China, like South Korea, will become a Christian country in the twenty-first century is no more than conjecture, the assertion that China is thoroughly open to Christian evangelism can be easily substantiated.

With the establishment of departments of religion at major universities, notably Beijing and Wuhan, the area of Christian studies as a subject of research and teaching is no longer confined to theological seminaries. Since the advent of reform and a more open policy in 1979, Christian theology has become a significant subject of inquiry at the most prestigious universities in China. As scholars holding Ph.D. degrees in Christian studies begin to make their presence known in the academic community, the impact on scholarship in the humanities and social sciences can be substantial. Moreover, reports of Christians' election to leadership positions in village and township enterprises, sporadic as they are, indicate that Christianity is well on its way to being fully accepted in parts of rural China, such as the Shandong Peninsula. These two developments, one in the confines of the ivory tower and the other at the grassroots of Chinese society, outline a wide spectrum of possibilities for the future of Christianity in socialist China.

The Buddhist Revival

From the larger perspective of cultural China, it is intriguing to note that on the island of Taiwan, despite the continuing encouragement of the top political leadership of Taiwan's Nationalist government, Christian evangelism reached its apex in the 1970s, when Taiwan's economy began to take off. Since then the Christian population on the island has remained at roughly 5 per cent. The situation is comparable to that of Japan, where Christian membership has remained steady at 3 per cent for decades. By contrast, the effervescence of Buddhist evangelism, especially the politically concerned and socially engaged Buddhist movements, must be recognized as one of the most significant features of the Taiwanese religious landscape. Self-styled as humanist Buddhists, the followers of Ciji, Xilai, and Fagu temples, which originated from and are rooted in the local Taiwanese culture, have made their *dharma,* their religious teaching, thoroughly international and profoundly influential in overseas Chinese communities. In Taiwan, these Buddhist organizations function as richly endowed economic institutions, broadly entrenched educational systems, well-connected mass media networks, and widely recognized centers of political influence.

The political culture in socialist China has not allowed similar developments on the mainland, but the upsurge of interest in Buddhism, in the proliferation of both the *sangha* (monastic orders) and lay communities, is notable. Virtually all famous temples in the Buddhist sacred mountains have been restored. The "incense fire," to use a local expression, is spreading throughout the land. Even in the early stage of the reform and open period, Buddhist monastic orders began to attract voluntary monks from many sectors of Chinese society, including college students. My personal experience some years ago is indicative of this Buddhist revival:

I was struck during my own pilgrimage to the Buddhist holy land honoring the "Goddess of Mercy," Putuo, in the autumn of 1980 before it was open to tourists, that the rise of the Buddhist sangha as the center of learning was on the horizon. The financial support from Chinese abroad helped to set up the infrastructure for Buddhist education and to recruit novices beyond the quota sponsored by the government there. Yet, the commitment of the old monks who voluntarily returned to teach the dharma after more than a decade of personal hardship was the single most important factor for re-introducing the Buddhist way of life to the Chinese youth.

After I, together with hundreds of others, attended an evening ceremony of sutra chanting at one of the large temples in Putuo, I discussed the future prospects of Buddhist studies with the head monk. He confided to me that since there were so many requests for instruction from brilliant young minds all over China, he had no doubt that a Buddhist renaissance was in the offing. "How do you know that a government functionary doing his routine job in a small office in Beijing does not, through his personal devotional effort, set the dharma wheel turning?" These were his parting words to me.[2]

If we include in our survey the pilgrims, especially woman devotees, who are not only an integral part but also the most vibrant presence on the religious scene at Putuo, the future of Buddhism indeed seems bright.

Putuo, the holy land of the Buddhist devotional sects, may be exceptional, but the "incense fire" is burning brilliantly in scores of other sacred sites as well, notably Wutai, Emei, and Tiantai. Buddhist lay organizations, led by the charismatic and respected literary figure Zho Puchu, have been instrumental in making the Buddhist message widely known in all walks of life and in all tourist spots. The government leadership in Beijing is very aware of the political importance of the voice of the *dharma* in forging alliances with compatriots in Taiwan, East Asia, Southeast Asia, the Asia-Pacific region, and the world beyond. For example, close collaboration between the Chinese Buddhist associations in North America and the famous temples in China has significantly sensitized Chinese-Americans to local conditions in China, prompting them to make contributions to alleviate illiteracy, poverty, and unemployment in selected provinces.

Against numerous vital signs of the Buddhist revival, Hu Shi's lament about the "Indianization" of the Chinese soul, a lament arising from the emphasis on modernization defined in terms of wealth and power, may appear to be the lonely cry of an outmoded positivist. Yet, undeniably, the mentality of the political leadership and Chinese intellectual elite is positivistic, scientistic, materialistic, utilitarian, and, by and large, deaf to religious matters. Post-reform China is ruled by technocrats trained in the former Soviet Union and East European countries. All but two major universities in China are headed by "scientists" with a strong emphasis on engineering. Engineers occupy a disproportionately large segment of the emerging top leadership in the central government as well. The tendency to manage the country through techniques of social engineering is strong, while the importance of religion as a source of cultural competence and ethical intelligence as well as spiritual values has yet to be recognized.

Tibet: Two Realities

Tibet is a case in point. The same geographic area, the same history, the same culture, and the same race turn out to be radically different realities when seen through different lenses. There is a great gap between the Tibet that is on the Chinese geopolitical map and the Tibet in Western ethico-religious consciousness. Chinese intellectuals at home and abroad share Beijing's concern that Western powers, especially the United States, wish to use Tibet to contain China during the process of unification. They also share Beijing's fear that an independent Tibet would trigger a movement by the minorities in the northwest to seek separate national identities. Furthermore, the scientistic mentality of the top political leadership is so insensitive to religion as an inalienable part of the culture of modern civilization that it automatically interprets Western support for the Dalai Lama as a strategy to discipline China in the international arena or a conspiracy to undermine Chinese political leadership at home.

President Jiang Zemin was acutely aware of the 4 T's—Trade, Taiwan, Tiananmen, and Tibet—during his visit to the United States in October 1997, but he and his advisors were truly surprised that the protests on behalf of Tibet generated the strongest feeling among non-Chinese American groups. During the Clinton-Jiang joint news conference in the People's Hall in July 1998, the Chinese president expressed genuine bewilderment over the allure of Lamaism for Western youth. Jiang did acknowledge, however, the need to know more about the situation. This may augur an openness to the possibility of a dialogue.

Actually, an attitudinal change is a precondition for any meaningful communication between Beijing and Dharmasala, the seat of the Dalai Lama and the Tibetan government in exile. Tacit understanding, if not agreement, is required on such queries as: Where is Tibet? How do we interpret Tibetan history? What is Tibetan culture? Who are the Tibetans? None of these questions is easily answerable. We must reexamine the earlier assertions about Tibet as being and having the same geography, the same history, the same culture, and the same race as China. To take geography as an example: the Chinese assumption of the Tibetan plateau is at odds with the claim of the Tibetan government in exile, a claim that includes at least Qinghai and a substantial part of Sichuan.

The Chinese insistence that as a precondition for negotiation the Dalai Lama renounce the concept of Tibet as an independent state, and that the Tibetan government in exile and Taiwan establish no alliance of any kind, indicates clearly Beijing's geopolitical thinking. The idealized Tibetan self-definition that sees India as spiritual guru, China as political protector, and Mongolia as disciple is at odds with the Chinese perception that Tibet, an integral part of Chinese territory that was under imperialist influence for decades, is still the backwaters of modernization. While Beijing feels fully justified in its efforts to transform Tibet from an archaic, hierarchical, superstitious, and oppressive theocracy into a socialist autonomous state, the Tibetans in exile appeal to the international community, especially the liberal democratic countries in the West, to stop China's "cultural genocide."

The Dalai Lama's full and self-conscious endorsement of human rights, democratic polity, and science has yet to be recognized by the intellectual community in cultural China. The Tibetan intellectuals as well as others who are committed to the Tibetan course must begin to grasp the complex history of the Sino-Tibetan relationship, especially the chapters covering the Manchu Empire, the Republican era and the contemporary period prior to 1959, and the Tibetan situation since the Dalai Lama's departure. However, the burden is on

China to lift the veil of ignorance and explore the possibility of dialogue.

If China takes India as a reference society and Indian religious pluralism as a reference culture, China may begin to appreciate its indigenous spiritual resources, such as Mahayana Buddhism. This could bring about a renewed appreciation of religion as an integral part of the vibrancy of modern life. As a result, Tibet could assume an entirely different shade of meaning in Chinese political consciousness. If Tibet were no longer perceived as a threat to China's territorial integrity nor regarded merely as a tool of Western hegemonic powers, its cultural significance rather than its geopolitical position would feature prominently on the agenda. Indeed, in the Chinese order of things, Tibet could become a Buddhist holy land and a major center for international Buddhist studies. The Dalai Lama, far from being a political separatist, could be a Chinese spiritual teacher as well as a Tibetan Buddhist leader. To transform this wishful thinking into a practicable policy, Beijing need not abandon its psychology of suspicion, its wariness of American conspiracy, or its apprehension of any geopolitical groundswell that might undermine China's territorial integrity.

Islam in China

The Islamic situation may give us a clue. The estimated 15 million Muslims in China are divided into two distinct groups: the thoroughly Chinese Huihui and the non-Chinese-speaking minorities, ten ethnic groups of which the main one is the Uighurs. The Han majority Muslims (perhaps more than 10 million) significantly outnumber the total of the minorities. Although the origins of the Islamic presence in China can be easily traced to the seventh century and the first generation of the Prophet's followers, Islam has become an indigenous Chinese religion since the fourteenth century. As a faith community, a social consciousness, an ethical mode of conduct, a value-orientation, and a style of life, Islam has been fully integrated into the Chinese religious landscape, even though the complete translation of the Koran into Chinese did not appear until the twentieth century. Recent research on the Islamic-Confucian dialogue clearly demonstrates that in the seventeenth century a highly original synthesis of Islamic theology and neo-Confucian cosmology was accomplished.

This creative transformation of Islam into Chinese literary culture may have been why Islam was not subjected to anti-foreign sentiments as Christianity was in the nineteenth century. It is remarkable to note that while the introduction of Muslim culture in China was not at all connected with Western imperialism, Islam was identified as a significant motive force for rebellions against the central government in late imperial China.

Muslims, both Chinese- and non-Chinese-speaking, are marked by their distinctiveness:

> Their social life centered around the mosque, their sense of the holy land symbolized by Mecca, and their personal faith directed toward Allah further help them to develop a separate cultural identity to which fundamentalist movements abroad may very well strike a sympathetic chord. The non-Chinese-speaking Muslims, mainly the Uighurs, with the added complexity of separate ethnic identity are more prone than Huis to express their Pan-Islamic sentiments.[3]

The upsurge of Sufi and Shiite activities in the Chinese Muslim communities certainly has far-reaching implications for the Chinese leadership, but China's close, if not intimate, relationships with Muslim countries in the Middle East as well as in Southeast Asia have enabled the socialist state to capitalize on its strength as a multi-lingual, multi-ethnic, and multi-religious civilization. After all, the Manchu dynasty, which ruled China for centuries (1644-1912), fully acknowledged its linguistic, ethnic, and religious pluralism by identifying Manchu, Chinese, Tibetan, and Mongolian as the four official languages.

Looking Ahead

Whether or not China will eventually become a religiously harmonious country largely depends on its attitude toward organized religions, mainly Christianity, Buddhism, and Islam. Issues of religious freedom, human rights, and public space for worship, prayer, and other activities characteristic of faith communities already loom large in Chinese political culture. As China is well on its way to becoming an active member of the international society, the political significance of religion will continue to be obvious.

Nevertheless, the quality of China's religious life will be substantially shaped by more personal and inward practices, specifically the art of healing, which involves such exercises as *qigong* (breathing technique), *taiji* (shadow boxing), herbal medicine, and acupuncture. This cultivation of the inner self, through mental and physical discipline of the vital energy *(qi)* inherent in the body, predisposes one to lend a sympathetic ear to a way of life commonly labeled Daoist (Taoist), a way of life that cherishes values of peace, harmony, balance, sympathy, rightness, and communion. If these values are deliberately cultivated by an ever-expanding circle of practitioners, the emergence of an aesthetic and ethical ethos that could underlie all religious practice is at least a possibility. Since more than 100 million Chinese of varying ages, social strata, walks of life, and cultural backgrounds are familiar with this approach to self-cultivation, there is a solid basis for further enhancing the efficaciousness of this art of healing.

My own impression, written some two decades ago, of the possibility of transforming this art of healing into a pervasive aesthetic and ethical ethos is still relevant:

[If] one personally journeys to sacred mountains such as Taisha, Qingchengshan, and Laoshan, one will immediately witness a phenomenon that gives special meaning to these places: pilgrimage disguised as tourism. We see subtle signs of worship every step of the way. Small shrines, sometimes barely visible from the mountain paths, come alive with simple but varied decorations. Major temples are always crowded with devotees and onlookers. Daoist priests are often at the center of attention; the surrounding students who ask them questions are eager to learn about every aspect of the tradition. The demand for introductory texts is so great that publishing large editions of Daoist precepts by the National Daoist Association has become a profit-making enterprise. The potential for growth in the Daoist book market is substantial. The manuals for *taiji* and *qigong* [shadow boxing and breathing techniques] alone are sufficient to sustain good business for some small publishing houses. As the Daoist message spreads through oral transmission as well as the printed word, an increasing number of Chinese will learn to be human through the Daoist way.[4]

Unfortunately, the caveat is that, as the result of the market economy, ocean waves of commercialism have recently engulfed virtually all sacred sites. Cultural tourism substantially defines the functions of temples and roles of priests.

Still, faith in the compassion of heaven, the sanctity of the earth, and the intrinsic worth of being human in our ordinary daily existence enables Chinese people to relate deliberately and meaningfully to family, society, nation, and the global community. They are empowered by a pragmatic idealism that enables them to see that a fruitful interaction between self and community, a sustainable and harmonious relationship between human species and nature, and mutual responsiveness between humanity and heaven are possible and practicable. Their faith and pragmatic idealism may not be enough to safeguard the dignity of the person, the authenticity of the fiduciary community (the Confucian ideal of a community of trust[5]), and the truth and reality of the transcendent. But as the overall pattern of symbolic control dominated by the rhetoric of class struggle, dictatorship of the proletariat, bureaucratic centralism, and continuous revolution fades away, the quest for meaning at all levels will give rise to a new religious consciousness with great potential for the cultivation of a common creed in a pluralistic modern society.

Political Islam in National Politics and International Relations

Abdullahi A. An-Na'im

The current regressive and antagonistic manifestations of political Islam are the product of a specific set of factors that are both internal and external. Their negative consequences affect Islamic as well as non-Islamic societies, particularly in view of the fast-growing interdependence among countries and regions of the world. Accordingly, both internal and external actors, non-Islamic and Islamic societies, must develop strategies of response.

Political Islam can be broadly defined as the mobilization of Islamic identity in pursuit of particular objectives of public policy, both within an Islamic society and in its relations with other societies. At that level of generality, political Islam is neither new, nor transient, nor necessarily negative. In fact, the mobilization of Islamic identity toward such goals can be seen as integral to the legitimate right of Muslim peoples to self-determination. The questions have to do

---

Abdullahi A. An-Na'im is a professor of law at Emory University in Atlanta, Georgia, where he also teaches a seminar on "Islam and Politics" in the Graduate Division of Religion. He is the author of *Toward an Islamic Reformation: Civil Liberties, Human Rights, and International Law* (Syracuse University Press, 1990). Dr. An-Na'im is a noted scholar of Islam and human rights and of human rights in cross-cultural perspective.

with what the legitimate objectives of public policy are and how these objectives are implemented.

Competing perceptions of Islamic identity lead to varying conceptions of an Islamic right to self-determination, and so there are bound to be different approaches to exercising this right. The fact that in a given setting a particular sense of Islamic identity is mobilized in pursuit of specific objectives of public policy should not be accepted as necessarily inevitable or permanent. Alternative perceptions of Islamic identity can be mobilized to serve other public-policy goals.

In characterizing current manifestations of political Islam as regressive and antagonistic, I refer primarily to the policies and practices of fundamentalist regimes in Afghanistan, Iran, Pakistan, and Sudan, and to the present and projected consequences of similar Islamic movements seeking political power in countries like Algeria and Egypt today.[1] But other manifestations of political Islam can be seen in the authoritarian "traditional" regimes of Saudi Arabia and the Gulf states, as well as in certain cultural institutions and political processes in other Islamic countries. For example, the fact that the legitimacy of the present monarchies of Jordan and Morocco is to some extent founded on an Islamic religious rationale reflects another aspect of political Islam. So does the role of certain religious institutions in the political and cultural affairs of many Islamic countries, from al-Azhar University in Egypt to Pusat Islam (National Fatwa Council) in Malaysia. I am critical here of the fundamentalist variety of political Islam as a general phenomenon with numerous variations,[2] but I also have some concerns about the more traditional forms of political Islam. Yet I see in the existence of such a variety of approaches a clear indication of the possibilities of transformation that will be suggested later in this essay.

By focusing on Islamic fundamentalism, I am not suggesting that this is the only or even primary cause of all the problems of Islamic societies. On the contrary, the emergence of fundamentalist movements everywhere can be seen as an outgrowth of deeper societal crises. Secular regimes and ideologies have also caused very serious problems for societies and regions. From Egypt under Nasser three decades ago to Iraq under Saddam Hussein today, secular nationalist projects have brought untold suffering to the people of certain states and have undermined the security and well-being of others beyond their borders. Moreover, an examination of fundamentalist Islam should take political Islam in broader regional and global context, both historical and contemporary. Nonetheless, I believe that recent developments justify a focus on the implications of fundamentalism for national politics and international relations.

I began by saying that the regressive and antagonistic manifestations of political Islam grew out of a concurrence of certain internal and external factors. To say this is not to imply a deliberate conspiracy to make this happen. Nor are the factors that might counteract these antagonistic manifestations likely to coalesce in a conspiracy of response. But human choices and actions on both sides of the issue will make a difference to the outcome, and they should be informed by a clear understanding of the role of both internal and external factors.

My purpose in arguing for shared understanding of the genesis and dynamics of fundamentalist political Islam is to promote coordination between internal and external responses. To call for such coordination is not to compromise Muslim people's right to self-determination, nor is it to concede the permanent hegemony of a particular foreign ideology and its models for individual and communal life. As I will emphasize, the internal dynamics of claims to self-determination, as well as external responses to those claims, should not be premised on a self-fulfilling prophecy of an inevitable "clash of civilizations." On the contrary, I will argue that sustainable and equitable self-determination can be realized today only through a deep appreciation of the interdependence of all human societies. Moreover, I believe that proclamations of the "end of history" in favor of one ideological and economic framework or another will probably lead to antagonistic counter-assertions.[3] As long as human beings continue to populate this planet, struggles for political participation and for economic and social justice will continue according to differing perceptions of individual and communal well-being. No single theory can possibly account for all the complexities in diverse societies.

In what follows I will first examine the relationship between political Islam and the politics of identity in Islamic societies, with a view to exploring possible alternative implications of political Islam for national politics and international relations. Next, I will look at the role of international relations in promoting competing forms of political Islam, both at home and abroad. Then, since an assumption of the unity of Islam and politics often underlies discussions of political Islam, I will examine the nature of that assumed unity, with a view to proposing an Islamic approach to secularism. In my conclusion, I will briefly consider the implications of what I have said here for national politics and international relations.

THE POLITICS OF IDENTITY

Several explanations have been given for the recent rise of fundamentalist political Islam. One is the clear failure of secular national projects to deliver on the promises of independence from colonial rule since the 1950s. A related explanation is the frustration of younger, educated generations—in an age of rising expectations—with the lack of political participation and diminishing opportunities for economic and social mobility in their societies. The failure of secular nationalist leadership and ideologies is also strongly associated in the Middle Eastern context with repeated defeats by Israel, which is totally and unconditionally supported, armed, and funded by the United States and other leading Western liberal democracies. This common perception of Western bias and bad faith undermines the credibility of liberal notions of democracy and human rights, which are perceived to be Western. At the same time, alternative Marxist or socialist ideologies are seen as theoretically discredited and practically abandoned by their primary proponents in the former Soviet Union and Eastern Europe. In any case, these ideological models have traditionally suffered in Islamic societies from being associated with militant atheism.[4]

Given this political and ideological vacuum, fundamentalists were able to present their vision of an Islamic alternative as the only viable, indeed "natural," ideology for Muslims everywhere.[5] Donning the mantle of exclusive religious legitimacy, fundamentalists are asking: How, after decades of political independence, can Islamic societies fail to assert their Islamic identity and to implement *Shari'a* (traditional formulations of Islamic law as a comprehensive legal and ethical system) as the divinely ordained way of life? Does not the Qur'an condemn those who fail to implement God's commands as infidels and hypocrites?

These and similar explanations are relevant. Yet we need to dig deeper. For example, why is an Islamic ideology presented in terms of enforcement of Shari'a through national politics at home and militant confrontation in international relations, even though this is contrary to the nature of Shari'a itself and, as we shall see, contrary to historical Muslim practice? Why is there so little critical examination within Islamic societies of traditional conceptions of Shari'a and their implications in the present context of pluralistic politics at home and interdependence abroad? Are there alternative visions of an Islamic ideology? If so, how can such alternatives be further developed and propagated?

As a Muslim from the Sudan, I appreciate the appeal of an Islamic ideology and the promise of being true to one's religious beliefs and deep-rooted cultural identity. But I can also see serious problems with historical formulations of Shari'a as a framework for national politics and international relations. For example, Shari'a principles prohibit the recognition of women and non-Muslims as full citizens of an Islamic state, and impose some serious limitations on their rights in the administration of criminal justice. Furthermore, some of the underlying assumptions of Shari'a are taken to legitimate direct violent action by militant groups in pursuit of their political objectives. Historical formulations of Shari'a also precluded Muslim recognition of the equal sovereignty of non-Muslim states, collectively called *Dar al-Harb*—the abode of those who are in a permanent state of war with *Dar al-Islam,* the territory of Islam.[6] But very few Muslims have shown awareness of these principles of Shari'a and their extremely serious political consequences. Does this mean that Islamic societies are locked into a course that will keep propelling them further away from the rest of the world?

I said earlier that political Islam—in the broader sense of the mobilization of Islamic identity in pursuit of certain public-policy objectives—is neither new, nor transient, nor necessarily negative. An Islamic identity has always been integral to Muslim politics, and will remain so as long as there are people who profess this faith. However, as we shall see, this did not traditionally mean the strict enforcement of Shari'a by the state, or a condition of permanently hostile relations with non-Muslim societies, as proposed by Islamic fundamentalists today. In this light, fundamentalist movements should be seen as simply one form of political Islam, rather than the only way in which Muslims who take their faith seriously can relate that faith to their politics.

What is at issue, then, is the particular content of the Islamic identity that is being asserted. In the sort of fundamentalist political Islam practiced today in countries like Iran and Sudan, being Muslim requires not only the strict enforcement of Shari'a by the state but also the legitimation of particular methods of collective action against internal dissent or external threat. According to this view, Muslim dissidents are to be severely repressed and punished as heretics and traitors to the community, and the non-Muslim other should be treated with intense suspicion and violent hostility. All of this is said to be required by the practice of Shari'a as the divinely ordained way of life.

The Many Dimensions of Identity

I suggest that a viable response to fundamentalist political Islam can be based on the possibility of a more flexible conception of identity and religious piety, one that is tolerant of diversity and open to cooperation with the non-Muslim other. The theoretical framework that I propose for this transformation of Islamic identity is the "contingency and negotiability" of identity in general.

Identity is of central importance in the politics of most human societies. Although some of its dimensions are more formative than others, individuals or communities are never defined by a single dimension of their identity.[7] This multi-dimensional view of identity raises such questions as, Which dimension of identity is more important than others at a given time or in relation to a particular matter? Which dimension is taken to be dominant, by whom and in which context? That is, while expressions of identity are negotiable and contingent, and some may prevail over others at certain stages in relation to one matter or another, there is always room for human judgment and choice among a range of available options. Moreover, judgment and choice apply not only to the *forms* of expression of identity that people exhibit but also to their *content*.

Like anyone else, a Muslim today might identify himself or herself as a citizen of a particular country, the holder of a certain professional or occupational position, a spouse and a parent, and numerous other things, all at once. At a given point in a person's life, he or she may believe that being a Muslim should condition other aspects of life in ways that influence public policy as well as private behavior. A person may also choose not to assert an aspect of his identity. Being a parent, for instance, may be considered irrelevant in a professional setting, though parenthood may well be a fundamental and very important aspect of a person's identity. The point here is that a person may de-emphasize one aspect of his identity and emphasize another in the interest of some desirable public-policy objective, such as the need to promote national unity and peace in time of unrest. As argued by Francis Deng, for example, much of the present civil war in Sudan and its serious consequences to the whole region can be seen in terms of whether northern Sudanese wish to identify as African or Arab, Muslims or non-Muslims. A national identity able to accommodate the wide diversity of the population could bring this protracted and violent conflict to a peaceful conclusion.[8]

Given the multiplicity, contingency, and negotiability of identity, what motivates people to emphasize one dimension over others? Which aspects of their identity do people associate with issues of governance and public policy, as distinguished from purely private matters? How did the specific formulation of Islamic identity that lends credible political support to the current regressive and antagonistic forms of fundamentalism come about? In my view, the factors that condition these choices include (a) perceptions of risk and benefits, (b) perceptions of the attitudes of other parties, internal or external, to the constant "negotiation of identity," and (c) confidence in the viability of alternative options.

But there is certainly more to the process than purely subjective considerations of identity. Local or specific factors of various kinds—political, economic, sociological, cultural—have influenced the emergence of different facets of political Islam. The best way to try to understand the history and dynamics of particular groups in relation to other groups would of course be a detailed study of each case in its context. In view of space limitations, and the fact that much work has already been done in this field,[9] I will attempt here only a brief outline of a perspective for examining fundamentalist political Islam.

Elements of an Approach

One way of understanding the dynamics of fundamentalist groups in various countries is to view them as "social movements."[10] Social movements are defined by Sidney Tarrow as "collective challenges by people with common purposes and solidarity in sustained interaction with elites, opponents and authorities."[11] They combine cultural, ideological, and organizational strategies to mount and sustain collective action among participants who lack more conventional resources and explicit programmatic goals. Leaders may be able to mobilize a consensus around a recognition of common interests, but that will not result in the creation of a social movement unless they manage to tap deeper-rooted feelings of solidarity or identity. Tarrow comments, "This is almost certainly why nationalism and ethnicity—based on real or 'imagined' ties—or religion—based on common devotion—have been more reliable bases of movement organization in the past than social class."[12]

Clearly, this sort of analysis can shed light upon the emergence of Islamic fundamentalist groups in various countries. However, since people may reach divergent conclusions about the implications of political Islam, whether in general or in relation to specific issues, it is crucial to encourage the widest possible debate, subject to appropriate safeguards. The best approach to understanding and responding to Islamic fundamentalism should include, it seems to me, the following elements:

1. There must be clear acknowledgment of participants' right to self-determination in terms of their perception of Islamic identity, *but subject to the safeguarding of the right of all other citizens* to the same. That is, fundamentalists are both entitled to, and obliged to respect, the full benefits of democratic principles and human-rights protection. Genuine affirmation of this entitlement and obligation by all sides would begin to address the most objectionable aspects of Islamic fundamentalists' ideology and practice, such as their views on the status and rights of women and religious minorities and their willingness to use terrorist methods in pursuit of their objectives.

2. But since compliance with this principle cannot be left to the discretion of the participants, there is a strong need for credible enforcement. This should include, in my view, (a) protecting the free-

dom of expression and association so as to promote a strong and active public opinion, (b) supporting the work of non-governmental organizations, (c) safeguarding the independence of the judiciary, and (d) ensuring official compliance with the rule of law.

3. There should be an internal discourse within Islamic societies about the nature of the relationship between Islam and politics. For my part, I would focus attention on the need to redefine the nature and implications of Islamic identity in the modern context, rather than dispute the right of Muslim peoples to exercise their right to self-determination in these terms.

4. Such internal discourse must be firmly based on the realities of global power relations. And it must be supplemented by a cross-cultural dialogue with non-Islamic societies about economic, political, security, and other concerns.

In regard to this fourth point, let us look now at the reciprocal relationship between international relations and national politics. Certain attitudes and patterns of behavior by foreign governments tend to generate corresponding attitudes and patterns at the national level, while attitudes and patterns of behavior seen in national politics can similarly influence international relations.

SELF-FULFILLING PROPHECIES IN WORLD POLITICS

The relationship between international relations and the politics of Islamic societies is often expressed in terms of two polar views: either that developments in Islamic politics are merely reactions to Western domination, or that anti-Islamic attitudes in Western international politics are merely reactions to the oppressive national politics and anti-Western attitudes of Islamic societies. "Human rights" and "democracy," for instance, are said by one side to be Western impositions on Islamic societies; on the other side, the failure of Islamic countries to live up to these standards is said to cause negative attitudes toward those countries in Western and other international circles.

There is of course some truth in both of these views, but the real reciprocal nature of the relationship is lost in what Lawrence Davidson describes as "pointing fingers at each other and accentuating each other's aggressive action."[13] Since this relationship is reciprocal, change on one side can encourage change on the other. In other words, in addition to these mutually negative attitudes, an alternative dynamic of mutually positive attitudes must also be possible. There is a choice between positive and negative self-fulfilling prophecies.

The Negative Side

When certain Islamic societies are presented as the embodiment of oppression, aggression, brutality, fanaticism, and medieval backwardness, their presumed irrationality and hostility become the basis for Western attitudes toward all Islamic countries. These negative Western attitudes draw upon the militantly antagonistic ideology and practices of Islamic fundamentalists in different parts of the Muslim world, only to be cited by those groups in order to reinforce and validate their antagonistic ideology and practices. The unavoidable outcome of this vicious cycle of demonization and counter-demonization of the "other" as the permanently hostile "alien" is the fulfillment of that prophecy.

Take for example the highly influential "clash of civilizations" thesis powerfully presented by Samuel Huntington through several avenues since the early 1990s. In his book on the subject, political Islam is introduced as "an immediate problem to Europe."[14] The German chancellor and French prime minister are said to have agreed with the secretary general of NATO in 1995 that "Islamic fundamentalism was 'at least as dangerous as communism' had been to the West," and a " 'very senior member' of the Clinton administration" is quoted as saying that Islam is "the global rival to the West."[15] This type of characterization leads to a view that "something very much like war is underway," and to a prediction of "cold war or even cold peace" between Islam and the West.[16] However, in my view, while "evidence" to support this view can be found in the violent rhetoric of Islamic fundamentalists, evidence to the contrary can also be found. As I see it, the question is one of orientation and theoretical premise; there is a pressing need to analyze *all* the available evidence in its proper context.

It is instructive to see that, in speaking about a conflict between two different versions of what is right and what is wrong, Huntington comments: "So long as Islam remains Islam (which it will) and the West remains the West (which is more dubious), this fundamental conflict between two great civilizations and ways of life will continue to define their relations in the future even as it has defined them for the past fourteen centuries."[17] In my view, the very notion of reducing complex and heterogeneous regions of the world to "Islam" and "the West" is profoundly problematic from a social-science point of view, especially when it is supposed to characterize relations over fourteen centuries. To suggest that Islam has not changed and will not is simply not true to the historical experience of Muslim peoples from sub-Saharan Africa to Southeast Asia. It assumes a grossly simplified and static "definition" of Islam that nobody has the right to make, including Muslim communities themselves. Moreover, to speak of "the West" as the necessarily antagonistic counterpart of Islam not only compares a religious tradition to a geopolitical region but also is empirically difficult to substantiate. How can one speak of "the West" as a monolithic unit at the end of a century during which Western powers have fought *exclusively among themselves* what were by far the most destructive and savage wars in human history?

Several Western authors have clearly articulated the negative side of the "self-fulfilling prophecy" analysis. According to one of them, "our shortsightedness achieves exactly what it fears: the continued encouragement of Islamist tendencies and their radicalization."[18] Another said: "Today, some Americans and Middle Easterners (including some Islamic fundamentalists) have come to share similar views of each other as violent enemies. The hostile aspects of their mutual history dominate perceptions and postures of and toward one another. For those who see the relationship this way, violence is a self-fulfilling prophecy."[19] Jochen Hippler concluded a discussion of perceptions of the "Islamic threat" and Western foreign policy by saying: "A self fulfilling prophecy does not have to be original or sensible to have disastrous consequences. If we extol a culturally defined racism as the leitmotif of our foreign policy, we should not be surprised when other cultures consequently encourage isolationist tendencies and anti-Western confrontation."[20] Finally, and most significantly for my purpose, here is a point made by Andrea Lueg:

Certainly, not all elements of the stereotyped fear of the Islamic threat have been invented unaided. In Islamic societies examples of aggression, repression, fanaticism and so on are indeed to be found. But our perception of Islam as "the enemy" still has little to do with reality, because only certain *aspects* of reality are used to cement our clichéd images. Of course criticising this image-building does not mean accepting all aspects of Islamic societies without criticism. On the contrary: dismantling the image of "the enemy" is virtually a pre-requisite for a constructive critique.[21]

The Positive Side

In highlighting this negative side of the coin, my purpose is to emphasize the equally valid reality of the positive side of the self-fulfilling prophecy. I base this on two main elements. First, I would note that this positive side already exists, that peaceful cooperation between Islamic and Western societies and countries is the rule rather than the exception. There are more than 1.2 billion Muslims around the world, constituting the majority of the population of about fifty countries in Africa and Asia. The vast majority of these Muslims and their states are engaged in daily trade and other economic activities, peaceful political relations, and cultural exchange with Western countries. If mutual antagonism and hostility are to become the norm in relations between Islamic and Western societies, civilization as we know it in the world today will be simply impossible.

The second and equally important element of my argument for peaceful and constructive international relations has two components. First, there is the need for candid acknowledgment of the problematic aspects of relations between Islamic and Western societies, and for clear understanding of the causes. Second, each society and country needs to address its part in the underlying causes of conflict. Self-criticism and internal changes are imperative on both sides if existing levels of peaceful co-existence and cooperation are to be maintained and extended. For every human society, conflict, both within itself and in its relations with other societies, is a permanent and normal part of life. What is at issue is whether a society is able to mediate and manage conflict or allows it to intensify into violent confrontation. The fact that peaceful and cooperative relations exist now does not mean that violent confrontation will never happen, or even come to prevail as the normal pattern. Conversely, violent confrontation can be transformed into peaceful cooperation.

Each society and country has a choice: Will its relations with others be based on mistrust and violent confrontation or on trust and mediation of conflict? But the theoretical possibility of a choice is meaningless unless it is actually made through the country's political and social institutions and followed by concrete action. For a choice to be made in a legitimate and sustainable manner, there is need for the widest possible public debate and participation.

In this light I now turn to the relationship between Islam and politics as understood *within* Islamic societies. Without clarification of this relationship, I believe, genuine and lasting democratization and protection of human rights will not be possible in any Islamic country today. And without these there cannot be the sort of public debate and participation I believe is necessary in order for Islamic societies to choose the positive self-fulfilling prophecy of peaceful and cooperative relations with all human societies.

AN ISLAMIC APPROACH TO SECULARISM

Although the Islamic consciousness of a community certainly influences Muslim attitudes toward political authority, it is misleading to assert that Islam is the sole basis of the ethics and political culture of any human society, past or present. To begin with, much of what came to be accepted as Islamic norms and institutions was based on pre-Islamic practices. And as Islam spread throughout the Middle East, North Africa, and beyond, Muslim religious practice was also greatly influenced by local customs, political and legal institutions, and the like.[22] Today, moreover, the attitudes and behavior of Muslims are largely shaped by economic, security, and other concerns that require extensive interaction with non-Islamic societies. This is particularly important to note in view of the geographical and cultural diversity of Islamic societies today.[23] Nevertheless, the relationship between Islam and politics in Islamic societies is so strong that strict separation between the two is commonly believed to be neither desirable in principle nor possible in practice.

In this light, I am calling for a clarification of the relationship between Islam and the political authority in the modern state, rather than an attempt at either complete unity or total separation. More specifically, I am suggesting the elaboration of an approach to secularism that is informed by Islamic religious values, rather than an attempt to implement historical formulations of Islamic law (Shari'a) as such. Human reason and the accumulated wisdom of human experience can help us see that the Qur'an and Sunna (traditions of the Prophet) provide a broad general framework for the modern state under the rule of law, in accordance with principles of popular sovereignty and the political and legal accountability of the government and its officials. For this approach to be taken seriously, it must be shown to be more appropriate than the two presently competing models of (1) an Islamic state that enforces Shari'a and (2) strict separation of Islam and politics.

I fully accept the reality of a dynamic relationship between faith and the attitudes and daily behavior of Muslim individuals and communities; yet I caution against the great danger to both aspects if the two are fused. To unite faith (which pertains to the individual consciousness) and matters of politics, economy, and social life (which operate in the public domain of rights and obligations through legislation and executive action) will necessarily lead to trivializing and undermining the authenticity of belief and worship in the lives of believers. Such unification will also lead to violation of the rights and freedoms of individuals and groups, and will jeopardize vital interests of society and the state. Founding such public functions as legislation, the administration of justice, and executive action on perceptions of the strength or weakness of a citizen's religious conviction and practice will lead to competitive pretense among believers who are seeking to promote their mundane interests. In such a competition, subjective considerations of piety and religiosity will be confused with objective factors of making and implementing policy. This confusion will also adversely affect the rights and obligations of individuals and groups in relation to one another, and in their dealings with the organs and officials of the state.

"Islamic State": A Dubious Construct

As a matter of historical fact, moreover, the relationship between Islam and politics was never premised on the so-called Islamic state or the comprehensive application of Shari'a. True, ruling elites have usually sought Islamic legitimacy for their political power, but that can hardly define an "Islamic state" as a clear model that can be implemented today. Similarly, Shari'a always had its role in the life of Muslim individuals and communities, but that was by way of personal commitment and voluntary practice, rather than through coercive enforcement by the organs of the state.[24]

The notion of an "Islamic state" is an innovation developed by fundamentalists during the second half of the twentieth century. It is inherently inconsistent with the obvious fact that the divine sources of Islam cannot be understood and applied except through human reason and the concrete experience of Muslim societies. Since the outcome is necessarily a mixture of divine guidance and the human endeavor to understand and benefit from it, the institution that emerges from that combination is not a theocratic state; it is, rather, a human attempt to apply religious values to political, social, and economic affairs. Given the inevitable change in human affairs, especially in the modern world, a state that is informed by Islamic values must constantly evolve and adapt to new circumstances.[25] To call such a state "Islamic" is misleading because it contradicts the reality of the great diversity of Islamic religious and political thought; it is an attempt to monopolize religious legitimacy for a particular and necessarily limited human conception.

By the same token, traditional formulations of Shari'a can only be human and secular, because they are conditioned by the concrete experience of specific societies, rather than the direct expression of the perfection of divine revelation that is immune from human desire, whims, and error. Therefore, to speak of the enforcement of Shari'a by the state as a divine command is a contradiction in terms. Notwithstanding claims of regimes in Saudi Arabia, Iran, and Sudan, Shari'a cannot be *legitimately* enforced by a modern state because that would require human enactment of those principles into positive laws, which would contradict the essence of religious freedom of choice among competing interpretations of the Qur'an and Sunna. Shari'a can provide only general guidance for legislation, and not the actual content of laws.

In my view, the main problems in the relationship between Islam and politics derive from the profound connection between religion and history. The Qur'an, the Sunna, and the practices of the first

Muslim community were related to what went on in the societies of Mecca and Medina in the seventh century. That organic link was enhanced by the fact that the Qur'an was revealed in the Arabic language and was explained and applied by the Prophet in accordance with the nature of his society, in response to the human needs of his time and place, of seventh-century Arabia. Similarly, the use of the Qur'an and Sunna to develop principles and rules of Shari'a was equally conditioned by the historical context of the fast-expanding Islamic Empire.

Nevertheless, subsequent generations of Muslims took Shari'a to be synonymous with Islam itself, and the only legal, ethical, social, and political system that is valid from an Islamic point of view. That belief was enhanced by the continuity of historical experience from the first Muslim communities of Mecca and Medina to those in Iraq, Syria, and Egypt during the first and second centuries of Islam, when the methodology and main framework of Shari'a were elaborated. Now that the difference in time and place between those early Muslim societies and current ones has dramatically expanded, the question is whether that profound connection between Islam as a religion and the history of particular societies can be set aside. Is it possible to extrapolate the essence of the eternal message of Islam from the specifics of a particular time and place?

In Islamic fundamentalist discourse, it is claimed that the Prophet's state of Medina (A.D. 622-632) provides a historical model of a legitimate Islamic state that enforced Shari'a. This claim is wrong, because the nature of society and the state in that period was too special and specific to sustain comparison with any subsequent Islamic society or state. During those ten years in two small towns and a sparsely populated desert terrain of Arabia, Muslims were attempting to comply with the dictates of Islam voluntarily, as a matter of religious conviction, and in the actual presence of the Prophet, who inspired and guided their endeavors. There were no organs or institutions of the state that could legislate, execute policy, and adjudicate disputes. Moreover, that experience was accompanied by the continuation of divine revelation, and by further explanation by the Prophet until the end of his life.

To summarize this part of my argument, there is no escape from human agency in the conduct of the affairs of any society. In the case of Islamic societies, human agency is unavoidable in the interpretation of the Qur'an and Sunna, as well as in the development and implementation of state policies. Where the inherent fallibility of this unavoidable human agency is openly acknowledged, there will be opportunities for peaceful disagreement that can be regulated through appropriate political and legal institutions. That possibility is lost, however, when the reality of human agency is denied or disguised as an Islamic state applying divine Shari'a.

An Islamic vs. a European Approach to Secularism

In response to fundamentalist demands, many Muslim intellectuals today tend to advocate European conceptions of strict separation between Islam and political authority, legislation, and the administration of justice. This approach, which I will call secularism, is unlikely to succeed, because it fails to address the issue of its cultural legitimacy for the Muslim state. In particular, without addressing fundamentalist claims that they are seeking the establishment of an Islamic state to implement Shari'a, advocates of secularism will appear to be calling on their own societies to abandon their Islamic cultural and religious foundations in order to adopt philosophical models that have emerged from European experiences with Christianity and the Enlightenment. In practical political terms, moreover, secularism is untenable in Islamic societies, not only because it does not represent the experiential and emotional ties of these societies to their own religious and cultural values, but also because it came to Islamic societies in the dubious company of Western colonialism and postcolonial hegemony.

Advocates of secularism for Islamic societies are clearly motivated by objections to the agenda of Islamic fundamentalists; they fear the disastrous consequences of that form of political Islam for national politics and international relations. Ironically, however, their advocacy of secularism may in fact strengthen what they are opposing. If presented with European secularism as the only alternative to the so-called Islamic state and application of Shari'a, Islamic societies will clearly prefer the latter, however serious its conceptual faults and practical difficulties. Clear illustration of the risks of strict secularism can be seen in Iran in the drastic reversal since 1979 of every "secular" achievement of the previous regime, and in the fact that the Turkish army is the primary guardian of secularism more than seventy years after Atatürk's authoritarian effort to radically reformulate the Turkish state and society.[26] It is clear that in this age of self-determination, democracy, and the protection of human rights as a matter of international law, secularism cannot be forced on any Islamic society by an authoritarian regime. Whenever Islamic societies exercise their right to self-determination by choosing their own system of government, the outcome is unlikely to favor European conceptions of secularism.

In light of all this, I conclude that what must be done is to clarify and specify the relationship between Islam and political authority on the basis of an Islamic approach to secularism. Such an approach requires the best possible opportunities for public discourse and experimentation over time, in light of scholarly research to extrapolate the essence of Islamic values from the historical circumstances of early Islamic societies. From this perspective, the protection of basic human rights, especially freedom of belief, expression, and association, is an Islamic imperative—and not merely a requirement of international treaties—because these rights are prerequisites for the necessary discourse. The crucial safeguard throughout this process, as well as during the implementation of whatever models may emerge, is strict observance of the principle of pluralism and the protection of human rights.

Concluding Observations

I fully agree with Peter Berger's remark at the end of his essay in this volume that "those who neglect religion in their analyses of contemporary affairs do so at great peril." I take it that the analyses he refers to should inform and lead to action, because the "great peril" is to people's lives and well-being everywhere in the world today.

I do not subscribe to notions of global conspiracies, whether for or against the agenda of fundamentalist political Islam. Nonetheless, I am calling here for some coordination of internal and external responses to the regressive and antagonistic manifestations of this phenomenon. Human choices and actions on both sides of the issue will certainly make a difference to the outcome. Since the underlying causes and dynamics of fundamentalist political Islam can be identified, common strategies of response can also be developed.

In calling for coordination of response, I intend neither to compromise the right to self-determination of Muslim peoples, nor to concede the permanent hegemony of a particular foreign ideology and its models for individual and communal life. Rather, my intention is simply to emphasize that neither the internal dynamics of self-determination nor external responses to those aspirations should be premised on a self-fulfilling prophecy of an inevitable "clash of civilizations." On the contrary, I believe that sustainable and equitable self-determination can be realized in the modern context only through a profound appreciation of the organic unity and interdependence of all human societies.

I also believe that proclamations of the "end of history" in favor of one ideological and economic framework or another will probably lead to antagonistic counter-assertions. As human beings continue to struggle for political participation and for economic and social justice, they do so according to differing perceptions of individual and communal well-being, and they inevitably adopt different approaches toward the realization of these objectives. No single theory can possibly account for all the complexities facing all societies.

Instead of making such futile and counterproductive claims, all human societies should engage in internal discourse about their own problems, coupled with cross-cultural dialogue with other societies about issues of common concern. No human society is self-sufficient enough to be independent of other societies, or powerful enough to impose its will on them. Dialogue with an open mind and in a mutually respectful and understanding manner is the only way to achieve peaceful co-existence and cooperation.

Notes

CHAPTER 2

"Roman Catholicism"

GEORGE WEIGEL

1. For the text see *Origins* 9.17 (Oct. 11, 1979), 257-66.
2. *Origins* 25:18 (Oct. 19, 1995), 295.
3. Ibid.
4. Ibid.
5. *Veritatis Splendor,* #96.
6. Ibid., #97.
7. Cf. ibid., #101.

CHAPTER 3

"The Evangelical Upsurge"

DAVID MARTIN

1. Paul Freston, "Popular Protestants in Brazilian Politics," *Social Compass* 41/4 (1994): 537-70.
2. Ibid.
3. Paul Gifford, *Christianity and Politics in Doe's Liberia* (Cambridge: Cambridge University Press, 1993). See also Paul Gifford, "Prosperity: A New and Foreign Element in African Christianity," *Religion* 20 (1990): 373-88.
4. Grant Wacker, "Searching for Eden with a Satellite Dish: Primitivism, Pragmatism and the Pentecostal Character," in Richard Hughes, ed., *The Primitive Church in the Modern World* (Urbana and Chicago: University of Illinois Press, 1995), 139-66.

5. Steve Brouwer, Paul Gifford, and Susan Rose, eds., *Exporting the American Gospel: Global Christian Fundamentalism* (New York and London: Routledge, 1996).

CHAPTER 4
"Judaism and Politics"
JONATHAN SACKS

1. Milton Himmelfarb, *The Jews of Modernity* (New York: Basic Books, 1973), 359.
2. Quoted in Paul Mendes-Flohr and Jehuda Reinharz, eds., *The Jew in the Modern World* (New York: Oxford University Press, 1980), 104.
3. Sander Gilman, *Jewish Self-Hatred* (Baltimore: Johns Hopkins University Press, 1986), 2.
4. Seymour Martin Lipset, "A Unique People in an Exceptional Country," in Seymour Martin Lipset, ed., *American Pluralism and the Jewish Community* (New Brunswick, NJ: Transaction, 1990), 20.

CHAPTER 5
"Europe: The Exception?"
GRACE DAVIE

1. James O'Connell, *The Past and Future Making of Europe: The Role of Heritage and the Directions of Unity* (University of Bradford: Peace Research Report, No. 26, 1991).
2. Ibid., 9.
3. The European Values Study is a major cross-national survey of human values, first carried out in Europe in 1981 and then extended to other countries worldwide. It was designed by the European Values Systems Study group (EVSSG). Analyses of the 1981 material can be found in Stephen Harding and David Phillips, with Michael Fogarty, *Contrasting Values in Western Europe* (London: Macmillan, 1986); Jean Stoetzel, *Les Valeurs du Temps Présent: Une Enquête Européenne* (Paris: Presses Universitaires de France, 1983); Noel Timms, *Family and Citizenship: Values in Contemporary Britain* (Aldershot: Dartmouth, 1992); Sheena Ashford and Noel Timms, *What Europe Thinks: A Study of Western European Values* (Aldershot: Dartmouth, 1992); David Barker, Loek Holman, and Astrid Vloet, *The European Values Study 1981-1990: Summary Report,* published by the Gordon Cook Foundation on behalf of the European Values Group, 1992; and Peter Ester, Loek Holman, and Ruud de Moor, *The Individualizing Society: Value Change in Europe and North America* (Tilburg: Tilburg University Press, 1994). Barker, Holman, and Vloet includes a useful bibliography of the whole enterprise. A further restudy is planned for the turn of the century. The longitudinal aspects of the study enhance the data considerably.
4. The European Values Study reveals both the advantages and the limitations of survey methodology. These are discussed in the introductory sections of Harding

and Phillips, *Contrasting Values*.

5. Harding and Phillips, *Contrasting Values*, 29.

6. For a fuller picture at these data—essential for any detailed work—see Stoetzel, *Les Valeurs du Temps Présent;* Harding and Phillips, *Contrasting Values;* Barker, Holman, and Vloet, *The European Values Study;* and Ester, Holman, and de Moor, *The Individualizing Society,* together with the individual analysis for each European country involved in the survey. This statistical material can be complemented by a variety of case studies; good collections can be found in John Fulton and Peter Gee, eds., *Religion in Contemporary Europe* (Lewiston, Queenston Lampeter: Edwin Mellen Press, 1994), and Grace Davie and Danièle Hervieu-Léger, eds., *Identités religieuses en Europe* (Paris: La Découverte, 1996).

7. Harding and Phillips, *Contrasting Values*, 31-34.

8. One of the crucial questions raised by the EVSSG material concerns the future of European religion. Are we on the brink of something very different indeed: a markedly more secular twenty-first century? It is very difficult to tell how the relationship between believing and belonging will develop. Nominal belief could well become the norm for the foreseeable future; or the two variables may gradually move closer together as nominal belief turns itself into no belief at all. It is certainly the case that young people are less believing, in a conventional sense, than either their parents or their grandparents.

9. Harding and Phillips, *Contrasting Values*, 69-70.

10. Protestant Europe is undoubtedly more secular. A crucial question posed by the EVSSG data concerns the extent to which Catholic Europe will follow suit a generation or so later. Such a development seems increasingly likely.

11. Stoetzel, *Les Valeurs du Temps Présent*, 89-91.

12. Information (including statistics) about the Jewish communities in Western Europe can be found in Anthony Lerman, *The Jewish Communities of the World* (London: Macmillan, 1989); Règine Azria, *Le Judaïsme* (Paris: La Decouverte, 1996); and Jonathan Webber, ed., *Jewish Identities in the New Europe* (London/Washington: Littman Library of Jewish Civilization, 1994).

13. Estimates of the size of Europe's Muslim population are, inevitably, related to questions about immigration. Statistics relating to illegal immigration are particularly problematic.

14. Peter Clarke, "Islam in Contemporary Europe," in Stewart Sutherland et al., eds., *The World's Religions* (London: Routledge, 1988); Jørgen Nielsen, *Muslims and Western Europe* (Edinburgh: Edinburgh University Press, 1992), Bernard Lewis and Dominique Schnapper, eds., *Muslims and Europe* (London: Pinter, 1994); and Steven Vertovec and Ceri Peach, eds., *Islam in Europe* (London: Macmillan, 1997).

15. James Beckford, *Cult Controversies* (London and New York: Tavistock Publications, 1985), and James Beckford, ed., *New Religious Movements and Rapid Social Change* (London: Sage/UNESCO, 1986).

16. Oliver Leaman, "Taking Religion Seriously," *The Times,* London, 6 February 1989.

17. Steve Bruce, *Religion in the Modern World: From Cathedrals to Cults* (Oxford: Oxford University Press, 1996).

18. Peter Berger, *The Sacred Canopy: Elements of a Sociological Theory of Religion* (New York: Doubleday, 1967).

19. David Martin, *A General Theory of Secularization* (Oxford: Blackwell, 1979).

20. Bryan Wilson, *Religion in a Sociological Perspective* (Oxford: Clarendon Press, 1982).

21. Bruce, *Religion in the Modern World,* 230.

22. Ibid., 232.

23. Peter Berger, *A Far Glory: The Quest for Faith in an Age of Credulity* (New York: Doubleday, 1992).

24. David Martin, "The Secularization Issue: Prospect and Retrospect," *British Journal of Sociology* 42/3 (1991).

25. Indeed, in Bruce's recent account, even American exceptionalism is hardly necessary as the data are reconsidered to minimize the difference between Europe and the United States (*Religion in the Modern World,* 129-68).

26. Berger, *A Far Glory,* 32.

27. For an elaboration of these questions, see my forthcoming book *Religion in Modern Europe: A Memory Mutates,* to be published by Oxford University Press.

28. José Casanova, *Public Religions in the Modern World* (Chicago: University of Chicago Press, 1994).

29. Ibid., 211.

30. In many respects Casanova is building on the seminal work of Karel Dobbelaere in discerning the different strands within the concept of secularization. See especially Dobbelaere's 1981 article "Secularization: A Multi-Dimensional Concept," *Current Sociology* 29/2.

31. Casanova, *Public Religions,* 212.

32. José Pérez Vilariño, "The Catholic Commitment and Spanish Civil Society," *Social Compass* 44/4 (1997): 595-610.

33. Rational-choice theory offers a supply-side analysis of religious activity: the greater the choice of religious organizations, the greater the response will be. A lack of choice—for example, a dominant state church—leads to reduced activities. The outlines of the rational-choice debate can be found in issues of the *Journal for the Scientific Study of Religion* from 1994 onward.

34. Danièle Hervieu-Léger, *La religion pour mémoire* (Paris: Cerf, 1993).

35. Danièle Hervieu-Léger, *Vers un nouveau Christianisme* (Paris: Cerf, 1986).

36. Two excellent and very public examples can be found in the Requiem Mass held in Notre Dame after the death of President Mitterand and the state funeral given to Diana, Princess of Wales.

CHAPTER 6

"Quest for Meaning"

TU WEIMING

1. Tu Wei-ming, "The Religious Situation in the People's Republic of China Today: A Personal Reflection," in Frank Whaling, ed., *Religion in Today's World* (Edinburgh: T & T Clark, 1986), 290-91.

2. Ibid., 284-85.

3. Ibid., 281-82.

4. Ibid., 283-84.

5. See Tu Wei-ming, *Centrality and Commonality: An Essay on Confucian Religiousness* (Albany: State University of New York Press, 1989), 39-66.

CHAPTER 7

"Political Islam"

ABDULLAHI A. AN-NA'IM

1. As Sadik J. Al-Azm has clearly and authoritatively shown, it is appropriate to refer to these manifestations of political Islam as "fundamentalist" in an original sense, and not merely as a matter of recent translation of a term coined during the early twentieth century to describe an American Protestant movement. See his two-part article "Islamic Fundamentalism Reconsidered: A Critical Outline of Problems, Ideas and Approaches," *South Asia Bulletin* 13 (1993): 93-121, and 14 (1994): 73-98.

2. See Lawrence Davidson, *Islamic Fundamentalism* (Westport, CT: Greenwood Press, 1998), 66.

3. I am referring here to two books: Samuel P. Huntington's *The Clash of Civilizations and the Remaking of the World Order* (New York: Simon and Schuster, 1996), to be mentioned later, and Francis Fukuyama's *The End of History and the Last Man* (New York: Free Press, 1992). Without discussing it in this paper, I am objecting to Fukuyama's claim that we may be witnessing the end of history, the end point of human ideological evolution, and the universalization of Western liberal democracy as the final form of human government.

4. See Davidson, *Islamic Fundamentalism,* 12-17.

5. See Joel Beinin and Joe Stork, *Political Islam* (Los Angeles: University of California Press, 1997).

6. For a discussion of these matters see my book *Toward an Islamic Reformation: Civil Liberties, Human Rights, and International Law* (Syracuse, NY: Syracuse University Press, 1990).

7. For recent discussions of identity see, for example, Terrell A. Northrup, "The Dynamics of Identity in Personal and Social Conflict," in Louis Krisberg, Terrell A. Northrup, and Stuart J. Thorson, *Intractable Conflicts and Their Transformation* (Syracuse, NY: Syracuse University Press, 1989), 17-20 and 32-36; and Jurgen Habermas, "Citizenship and National Identity: Some Reflections on the Future of Europe," *Praxis International* 12 (1992): 1-12. On social identity and group identity see Will Kymlicka, ed., *The Rights of Minority Cultures* (Oxford and New York: Oxford University Press, 1995), 161-64.

8. Francis M. Deng, *War of Visions: Conflict of Identities in the Sudan* (Washington, DC: Brookings Institution, 1995).

9. There is a wealth of recent scholarship discussing this phenomenon in relation to individual movements and countries, or in terms of specific issues. Besides the previously cited Beinin and Stork, *Political Islam,* and Davidson, *Islamic Fundamentalism,* recent books on the subject include: Scott R. Appleby, ed., *Spokesmen for*

the Despised: Fundamentalist Leaders of the Middle East (Chicago: University of Chicago Press, 1997); John L. Eposito and John O. Voll, *Islam and Democracy* (New York: Oxford University Press, 1996); Hussin Mutablib and Taj ul-Islami Hashmi, eds., *Islam, Muslims and the Modern State: Case-Studies of Muslims in Thirteen Countries* (New York: St. Martin's Press, 1994); and John Ruedy, ed., *Islamism and Secularism in North Africa* (New York: St. Martin's Press, 1994).

10. See Edmund Burke III and Ira M. Lapidus, *Islam, Politics, and Social Movements* (Berkeley: University of California Press, 1988).

11. Sidney Tarrow, *Power in Movement: Social Movements, Collective Action and Politics* (Cambridge, England: Cambridge University Press, 1994), 3-4.

12. Ibid., 5.

13. Davidson, *Islamic Fundamentalism,* 74.

14. Huntington, *The Clash of Civilizations,* 204.

15. Ibid., 215.

16. Ibid., 217, 121.

17. Ibid., 212.

18. Jochen Hippler and Andrea Lueg, eds., *The Next Threat: Western Perceptions of Islam,* trans. Laila Friese (London: Pluto Press with Transnational Institute, 1995), 15.

19. Davidson, *Islamic Fundamentalism,* 74.

20. Hippler and Lueg, *The Next Threat,* 150.

21. Ibid., 8.

22. See Ira M. Lapidus, *A History of Islamic Societies* (Cambridge, England: Cambridge University Press, 1988), Part 1.

23. See, for example, Clifford Geertz, *Islam Observed: Religious Development in Morocco and Indonesia* (Chicago: University of Chicago Press, 1971).

24. Lapidus, *History of Islamic Societies,* 120-25.

25. Ali Abd al-Raziq, *al-Islam wa usul al-Hukm* (Arabic) (Cairo: Matbaat Misr, 1925); Abdelwahab El-Affendi, *Who Needs an Islamic State?* (London: Grey Seal Books, 1991).

26. Beinin and Stork, *Political Islam,* chap. 12.

Index of Names